CHRIST AND HIS THREEFOLD OFFICE

CHRIST AND HIS THREEFOLD OFFICE

John Flavel

Abridged by
J. Stephen Yuille

Reformation Heritage Books
Grand Rapids, Michigan

Christ and His Threefold Office
© 2021 by Reformation Heritage Books

All rights reserved. No part of this book may be used or reproduced in any manner whatsoever without written permission except in the case of brief quotations embodied in critical articles and reviews. Direct your requests to the publisher at the following addresses:

Reformation Heritage Books
3070 29th St. SE
Grand Rapids, MI 49512
616-977-0889
orders@heritagebooks.org
www.heritagebooks.org

Printed in the United States of America
21 22 23 24 25 26/10 9 8 7 6 5 4 3 2 1

Library of Congress Cataloging-in-Publication Data

Names: Flavel, John, 1630?-1691, author. | Yuille, J. Stephen, 1968-
Title: Christ and his threefold office / John Flavel ; abridged by J. Stephen Yuille.
Description: Grand Rapids, Michigan : Reformation Heritage Books, [2021]
Identifiers: LCCN 2021002129 (print) | LCCN 2021002130 (ebook) | ISBN 9781601788498 (paperback) | ISBN 9781601788504 (epub)
Subjects: LCSH: Jesus Christ—Person and offices.
Classification: LCC BT250 .F53 2021 (print) | LCC BT250 (ebook) | DDC 232—dc23
LC record available at https://lccn.loc.gov/2021002129
LC ebook record available at https://lccn.loc.gov/2021002130

For additional Reformed literature, request a free book list from Reformation Heritage Books at the above regular or email address.

Contents

Preface vii

1. The Excellence of the Subject 1
2. Christ's Essential Glory 9
3. The Covenant of Redemption 17
4. God's Admirable Love 27
5. Christ's Wonderful Person...................... 33
6. The Authority of the Mediator 44
7. The Consecration of the Mediator 52
8. The Nature of Christ's Mediation 60
9. The Prophet's Work of Revelation 69
10. The Prophet's Work of Illumination............... 78
11. The Nature and Necessity of Christ's Priesthood..... 88
12. The Priest's Oblation........................... 97
13. The Priest's Intercession........................107
14. A Full Satisfaction............................115
15. A Blessed Inheritance..........................125
16. The King's Spiritual Reign 133
17. The King's Providential Reign..................143

Conclusion 153

Preface

"One thing have I desired of the LORD, that will I seek after; that I may dwell in the house of the LORD all the days of my life, to behold the beauty of the LORD, and to enquire in his temple…. Hear, O LORD, when I cry with my voice: have mercy also upon me, and answer me. When thou saidst, Seek ye my face; my heart said unto thee, Thy face, LORD, will I seek" (Ps. 27:4, 7–8).

God created us in His image so that we might know and enjoy Him, but we broke away from Him and have lived with the isolation ever since. Mercifully, however, the story does not end there. The Son of God has drawn near to us in the incarnation. He came so close as to experience life in a fallen world, bear our sin and shame, and taste death for us. He was bruised, that we might be healed; humiliated, that we might be exalted; condemned, that we might be justified. At that moment of utter darkness and forsakenness on the cross, He purchased the enjoyment of God for us. In Christ, we now enjoy communion with God. In Christ, we "behold the beauty of the LORD."

This motif captured the attention of seventeenth-century English Puritan John Flavel.[1] The Holy Spirit led Flavel to a saving knowledge of Christ when he was a young man. Reflecting on his experience, he penned, "I studied to know many other things, but I knew not myself.... My body, which is but the garment of my soul, I kept and nourished with excessive care; but my soul was long forgotten, and had been lost forever...had not God roused it, by the convictions of His Spirit, out of that deep oblivion and deadly slumber."[2]

Flavel studied at University College in Oxford. After graduation, at age twenty-three, he entered his first pastorate at Diptford in the county of Devon. Six years later, he moved

---

1. For details of Flavel's life, see *The Life of the Late Rev. Mr. John Flavel, Minister of Dartmouth*, in John Flavel, *The Works of John Flavel* (London: W. Baynes and Son, 1820; repr., London: Banner of Truth, 1968), 1:i–xvi; and *Dictionary of National Biography*, ed. S. Lee (London: Smith, Elder, 1909). Flavel is the subject of the following PhD dissertations: Kawi Chang, "John Flavel of Dartmouth, 1630–1691" (University of Edinburgh, 1952); John Thomas Jr., "An Analysis of the Use of Application in the Preaching of John Flavel" (New Orleans Baptist Theological Seminary, 2007); Brian H. Cosby, "The Theology of Suffering and Sovereignty as Seen in the Writings and Ministry of John Flavel, c. 1630–1691" (Australian College of Theology, 2012); Nathan Thomas Parker, "Proselytization and Apocalypticism in the British Atlantic World—The Theology of John Flavel" (Durham University, 2013). In addition to these dissertations, there are several books on Flavel: Adam Embry, *Keeper of the Great Seal of Heaven: Sealing of the Spirit in the Life and Thought of John Flavel* (Grand Rapids: Reformation Heritage, 2011); J. Stephen Yuille, *The Inner Sanctum of Puritan Piety: John Flavel's Doctrine of Mystical Union with Christ* (Grand Rapids: Reformation Heritage, 2007); Brian H. Cosby, *John Flavel: Puritan Life and Thought in Stuart England* (Lanham, Md.: Lexington Books, 2014); Clifford B. Boone, *Puritan Evangelism: Preaching for Conversion in Late-Seventeenth Century English Puritanism as Seen in the Works of John Flavel* (Milton Keynes, UK: Paternoster, 2013).

2. Flavel, *Works*, 2:483–84.

to Dartmouth in the same county. He was a prolific preacher and writer (his collected works fill six volumes), and his pastoral influence extended well beyond his local congregation. He was "famous among the writers of his age,"[3] obtaining "more disciples" than John Owen or Richard Baxter.[4] The story is told of a young man who entered a London bookshop in search of plays. He was offended when the owner offered him a book by John Flavel. Incensed, he threatened to burn it. The owner eventually convinced the young man to take it. A month later he returned, exclaiming, "Sir, I most heartily thank you for putting this book into my hands. I bless God who moved you to do it, for it has saved my soul. Blessed be God, that I ever came into your shop!"[5]

Regrettably, Flavel's public ministry ceased for a time with the issuing of the Act of Uniformity in 1662.[6] For several years he continued to live in Dartmouth, meeting secretly with church members in order to preach the Scriptures and administer the sacraments. When the Oxford Act prohibited all nonconformist ministers from living within five miles of towns that sent representatives to Parliament, Flavel settled

---

3. John Galpine, "A Short Life of John Flavel," in *Flavel, the Quaker, and the Crown* (Cambridge: Rhwhymbooks, 2000), 13.

4. Anthony à Wood, *Athenae Oxonienses: An Exact History of All the Writers and Bishops Who Have Had Their Education in the University of Oxford* (New York: Lackington, Hughes, and Harding, 1820), 4:323.

5. Flavel, *Works*, 1:xiv.

6. In 1662, Parliament passed the Act of Uniformity, according to which all who had not received Episcopal ordination had to be reordained by bishops. In addition, ministers had to declare their consent to the entire Book of Common Prayer and their rejection of the Solemn League and Covenant. As a result, approximately two thousand ministers left the Church of England. They became known as "dissenters" or "nonconformists."

at a nearby village. His people ventured to hear him preach on the Lord's Day in private homes or wooded areas, and he slipped regularly into Dartmouth to visit them. One of their favorite places to gather was located on the Kingsbridge estuary, which was accessible during low tide.[7] This clandestine ministry continued until the political indulgence of 1687, when the authorities permitted him to resume his public ministry. He enjoyed this liberty until his death four years later at age sixty-four.

Flavel's influence continued after his death. Increase Mather notes in the preface to one of Flavel's works, "The worthy author of the discourse emitted herewith, is one whose praise in the gospel is throughout all churches. His other books have made his name precious and famous in both Englands."[8] His influence not only crossed oceans but spanned generations. Jonathan Edwards frequently quoted Flavel in his famous work *The Religious Affections*, and George Whitefield carried Flavel's works with him in his travels.[9]

At times Flavel is polemical and controversial in his writings.[10] More often than not, however, he is doctrinal and pastoral. This emphasis is seen in his twofold approach to preaching and writing: exposition and application. Flavel repeatedly follows this simple method, deriving his doctrines

---

7. A. G. Matthews and Edmund Calamy, *Calamy Revised: Being a Revision of Edmund Calamy's Account of the Ministers and Others Ejected and Silenced, 1660–1662* (Oxford: Oxford University Press, 1988), 200.

8. Flavel, *Works*, 4:16.

9. Quoted in Iain H. Murray, *The Puritan Hope: Revival and the Interpretation of Prophecy* (Edinburgh: Banner of Truth, 1971), 143.

10. This is evident, for example, in his treatises on antinomianism. See Flavel, *Works*, 3:413–591.

from Scripture and then encouraging his readers to pursue a heartfelt application of those doctrines to all of life. This *affective* theology places Flavel firmly within the realm of English Puritanism—what J. I. Packer calls "a spiritual movement, passionately concerned with God and godliness."[11]

Flavel's passion for God and godliness is particularly evident in the attention he gives to cultivating communion with God. He explains that there is such a thing as *positional* communion: "Thou art near, O LORD" (Ps. 119:151). The psalmist is not speaking here of God's presence of *essence*; that is, he does not suggest God is in some places more than others. On the contrary, God is present in all places at all times: "Whither shall I go from thy spirit? or whither shall I flee from thy presence? If I ascend up into heaven, thou art there: if I make my bed in hell, behold, thou art there" (Ps. 139:7–8). So what does the psalmist mean when he says, "Thou art near, O LORD"? He is referring to God's *gracious* presence—a privilege that belongs exclusively to His people.

Believers enjoy this nearness to God because of our union with Christ.[12] In Scripture, this *positional communion* is called *koinonia* (fellowship, partnership, participation). "God is faithful, by whom ye were called unto the fellowship of his Son Jesus Christ our Lord" (1 Cor. 1:9).

We are in fellowship (partnership/communion) with Christ's person. "The cup of blessing which we bless, is it not the communion of the blood of Christ? The bread which

---

11. J. I. Packer, *A Quest for Godliness: The Puritan Vision of the Christian Life* (Wheaton, Ill.: Crossway Books, 1990), 28.

12. For a full treatment of Flavel's understanding of union with Christ, see Yuille, *Inner Sanctum*.

we break, is it not the communion of the body of Christ?" (1 Cor. 10:16). Here Paul is speaking of the Lord's Supper. We participate in the blood of Christ when we bless the cup, and we participate in the body of Christ when we break the bread. This does not mean we physically drink Christ's blood and eat Christ's body. When Paul says we participate in the blood and body of Christ, he means we are one with Him by the Holy Spirit.

We are also in fellowship (partnership/communion) with Christ's benefits. "But of him are ye in Christ Jesus, who of God is made unto us wisdom, and righteousness, and sanctification, and redemption" (1 Cor. 1:30). We are one with Christ in His death and resurrection; therefore, we commune with Him in the fruits and benefits of His mediatorial work. This means, for example, that we have fellowship with His obedience (Rom. 8:1), His Spirit (Rom. 8:9–11), His Sonship (Rom. 8:14–16), His glory (Rom. 8:17), His suffering (Rom. 8:17), and His intercession (Rom. 8:34).

Positional communion is a tremendous encouragement to all believers because it speaks of our identity in Christ. It reminds us that we possess all things in Him. "For ye know the grace of our Lord Jesus Christ, that, though he was rich, yet for your sakes he became poor, that ye through his poverty might be rich" (2 Cor. 8:9).

In addition to this *positional* communion, there is—in Flavel's estimation—*actual* communion. As established above, God is always near to His people in Christ. This is God's gracious presence with us. But James declares, "Draw nigh to God, and he will draw nigh to you" (James 4:8). James does not deny the reality of *positional* communion but points to our experience of it. We must actively draw near to God, whereby He draws near to us. There are times when we feel God's presence, when He awakens those *graces* (e.g., faith, hope, love, joy) that He implanted in us at regeneration. By means of His Word and Spirit, He stirs these graces so that we know experientially that He is near. This is *actual* communion.

Christ declares, "Behold, I stand at the door, and knock: if any man hear my voice, and open the door, I will come in to him, and will sup with him, and he with me" (Rev. 3:20). Flavel believes that Christ is speaking of *positional* communion (union with Him) when He says, "I will come in to him, and will sup with him," whereas He is speaking of *actual* communion when He says, "and he with me."[13] As Flavel makes clear, "We can have no actual communion with the Father, Son, or Spirit, till we are first brought into a state of communion."[14] He adds, "All communion is founded in union; and where there is no union, there can be no communion."

Flavel defines *actual* communion as "a spiritual correspondence between Christ and the soul" as "God lets forth influences upon our souls, and we, by the assistance of His Spirit, make returns again unto Him."[15] But what exactly does it look like?[16]

God lets forth His greatness upon us, and we make returns in humility. "When I consider thy heavens, the work

---

13. These insights are gleaned from Flavel's treatise *England's Duty under the Present Gospel Liberty (1689)*, in Flavel, *Works*, vol. 4. It consists of eleven sermons based on Revelation 3:20.
14. Flavel, *Works*, 4:237.
15. Flavel, *Works*, 4:240.
16. Flavel, *Works*, 4:240–45.

of thy fingers, the moon and the stars, which thou hast ordained; What is man, that thou art mindful of him? and the son of man, that thou visitest him?" (Ps. 8:3–4). We are humbled (our "returns") in response to God's greatness (His "influences"). In response to our humbling, God lifts us up: "Humble yourselves in the sight of the Lord, and he shall lift you up" (James 4:10).

God lets forth His holiness upon us, and we make returns in repentance. "And one cried unto another, and said, Holy, holy, holy, is the LORD of hosts: the whole earth is full of his glory…. Then said I, Woe is me! for I am undone; because I am a man of unclean lips, and I dwell in the midst of a people of unclean lips" (Isa. 6:3, 5). We repent (our "returns") in response to God's holiness (His "influences"). In response to our repentance, God imparts peace: "I acknowledged my sin unto thee, and mine iniquity have I not hid. I said, I will confess my transgressions unto the LORD; and thou forgavest the iniquity of my sin" (Ps. 32:5).

God lets forth His goodness upon us, and we make returns in love. "This is a faithful saying, and worthy of all acceptation, that Christ Jesus came into the world to save sinners; of whom I am chief. Howbeit for this cause I obtained mercy, that in me first Jesus Christ might shew forth all longsuffering, for a pattern to them which should hereafter believe on him to life everlasting" (1 Tim. 1:15–16). We love (our "returns") in response to God's goodness (His "influences"). In response, God imparts love: "He that hath my commandments, and keepeth them, he it is that loveth me: and he that loveth me shall be loved of my Father, and I will love him, and will manifest myself to him" (John 14:21).

God lets forth His faithfulness upon us, and we make returns in faith. "I will never leave thee, nor forsake thee. So that we may boldly say, The Lord is my helper, and I will not fear what man shall do unto me" (Heb. 13:5–6). We trust (our "returns") in response to God's faithfulness (His "influences"). In response to our trust, God imparts comfort: "The LORD is my light and my salvation; whom shall I fear? the LORD is the strength of my life; of whom shall I be afraid?… Though an host should encamp against me, my heart shall not fear: though war should rise against me, in this will I be confident" (Ps. 27:1, 3).

These are examples of *actual* communion. In each instance, God communicates Himself to our souls (by means of His Word) so that we make returns to Him. These returns include the stirring of our affections: love, desire, delight, fear, sorrow, trust, and hope. When these affections are directed toward God, we draw near to Him and He draws near to us, meaning we enjoy *actual* communion with God. According to Flavel, this is "a felt presence of God which no words can make another to understand." We "feel that fountain flowing abundantly into the dry pits, the heart fills apace, the empty thoughts swell with a fullness of spiritual things, which strive for vent."[17]

We cultivate such communion with God by means of "the duties of religion"—praying, hearing the Word, and celebrating the sacraments.[18] By these duties the Holy Spirit "influences the graces" of God's people so that we "return the

---

17. Flavel, *Works*, 6:389.
18. Flavel, *Works*, 4:244.

fruits thereof in some measure to Him." These duties bring us into vital contact with the nature and works of God as revealed in Scripture.[19] More to the point, they bring us to Jesus Christ. Flavel declares, "Look on Him in what respect or particular you will; cast your eye upon this lovely object, and view Him in anyway; turn Him in your serious thoughts which way you will; consider His person, His offices, His works, or any other thing belonging to Him; you will find Him altogether lovely."[20] For starters, Christ is altogether lovely in His *person*: "The wonderful union and perfection of the divine and human nature in Christ, render Him an object of admiration and adoration to angels and men." Second, Christ is altogether lovely in His *offices*: "All the promises of illumination, counsel and direction flow out of the prophetic office. All the promises of reconciliation, peace, pardon, and acceptance flow out of the priestly office. All the promises of converting, increasing, defending, directing, and supplying grace flow out of the kingly office." Finally, Christ is altogether lovely in His *relations*. As redeemer, He delivers us from the depths of misery. As bridegroom, He unites us to Himself—we who are "deformed, defiled, and altogether unworthy." As advocate, He "pleads" our cause in heaven and "appears" for us in the presence of God.[21]

As we gaze on Christ's loveliness, we behold God's goodness, faithfulness, lovingkindness, holiness, and so on. The Holy Spirit lets forth these influences on our souls, and we make returns as our affections are stirred. For Flavel, this is

---

19. Flavel, *Works*, 4:240.
20. Flavel, *Works*, 2:215.
21. Flavel, *Works*, 2:218–22.

actual communion—"the life of our life, the joy of our hearts; a heaven upon earth."[22]

This communion by means of meditation on Christ's loveliness brings us to the present work: *Christ and His Threefold Office*.[23] Flavel sees the salvation of God's people as resting on the eternal covenant of redemption between God the Father and God the Son. In eternity, the Father and Son enter into a transaction to bring about the salvation of the elect. In time, the Son becomes a man, fulfills the covenant of works, and dies to pay the penalty incurred by His people under that covenant. Having done so, He returns to the Father, from where He sends forth the Holy Spirit to unite His people to Himself. By virtue of that union, they partake of the blessings of the covenant of grace.

In Flavel's mind, therefore, the fulfillment of the covenant of redemption is linked to two great unions.[24] The first is the hypostatical union between the divine and human natures in Christ, whereas the second is the mystical union between Christ and believers by means of the Holy Spirit. Flavel affirms that the first is the basis for the second. In other words, Christ must become one with us hypostatically in order for us to become one with Him mystically. Suffice it to say, Flavel believes that Christ "took or assumed the true human nature…into the unity of His divine person, with all its integral parts and essential properties; and so was made

---

22. Flavel, *Works*, 4:250.
23. This book abridges the first half of *The Fountain of Life*. Found in Flavel, *Works*, vol. 1, the original work is a collection of more than forty sermons, celebrating Christ from His preincarnate glory to His postresurrection glory.
24. Flavel, *Works*, 1:75.

(or, became) a true and real man by that assumption."[25] He believes that God the Son became a man "to qualify and prepare Him for a full discharge of His mediatorship, in the office of our prophet, priest, and king."[26]

Christ fulfills His prophetic office by "revelation" and "illumination,"[27] His priestly office by "oblation" and "intercession,"[28] and His kingly office by "subjection" and "governance."[29] "Salvation," says Flavel, "is revealed by Christ as a prophet, procured by Him as a priest, applied by Him as a king. In vain it is revealed, if not purchased; in vain revealed and purchased, if not applied."[30] Again, he remarks, "What Christ revealed as a prophet, He purchased as a priest; and what He revealed and purchased as a prophet and priest, He applies as a king."[31] Christ discharges His mediatorship as God-man in these three offices in order to secure the blessings that He lavishes on all those who are united with Him by the Holy Spirit.

The glory of Christ's threefold mediatorial office is the theme of this volume. Flavel's treatment of the subject is informed by Scripture and faithful to the historic creeds of the church. He is polemical when necessary and painstakingly detailed when he believes the truth is at stake. That said, his work does not fall within the traditional boundaries of systematic theology; rather, it is an act of adoration,

---

25. Flavel, *Works*, 1:73.
26. Flavel, *Works*, 1:80; see also 4:182–86.
27. Flavel, *Works*, 1:137.
28. Flavel, *Works*, 1:80.
29. Flavel, *Works*, 1:80.
30. Flavel, *Works*, 1:143.
31. Flavel, *Works*, 1:198–99.

constituting a series of meditations on "the transcendent excellency of Jesus Christ."[32] Above all else, Flavel wants us to "behold the beauty of the LORD," that we might enjoy communion with the living God. This, therefore, is how we are to read his work—thoughtfully, devotionally, and affectively. Our reading must be shaped by Flavel's own counsel to us: "To your work, Christian, to your work…. Whatever communion God and the soul maintains, it is in this way. Count all, therefore, but dross in comparison to that excellency which is the knowledge of Jesus Christ."[33]

—J. Stephen Yuille
Cambridge, Ontario
June 2020

---

32. Flavel, *Works*, 1:xvii.
33. Flavel, *Works*, 1:42.

1

The Excellence of the Subject

For I determined not to know any thing among you, save Jesus Christ, and him crucified.
—1 CORINTHIANS 2:2

The preceding verse contains the apostle's defense of his plain manner of preaching. It was not characterized by "excellency of speech or of wisdom," as he was not interested in gratifying people's curiosity with rhetorical devices or philosophical niceties. He gives his reason in this verse: "For I determined not to know any thing among you, save Jesus Christ, and him crucified." The apostle does not mean that he despised and condemned all other study and knowledge, but only so far as they stand in competition with (or opposition to) the study and knowledge of Christ. All other knowledge, however pleasant and profitable, is not worthy to be named in the same sentence with the knowledge of Christ. Therefore, the apostle resolves to make this knowledge the end and scope of his ministry. He applies himself to plain, common, and genuine language, more suited to pierce the heart and convince the conscience than to tickle the fancy. This is the meaning of the apostle's words, in which we should note three things.

First, the apostle mentions the subject of his preaching: "Jesus Christ." Christ is the center to which all the lines of his ministry are drawn. The apostle has spoken of many other subjects in his sermons and epistles, but it is all reducible to the preaching of Christ. This is the sweetest of all the subjects in the world. If there is anything on this side of heaven worthy of our time and study, it is this. Thus, he magnifies his preaching from the excellence of its subject.

Second, the apostle mentions one truth in particular: "him crucified." He focuses on this truth because he wants to address the prejudice raised against him on account of Christ's cross. "But we preach Christ crucified, unto the Jews a stumbling block, and unto the Greeks foolishness" (1 Cor. 1:23). Moreover, this subject best suits the apostle's purpose in writing, which is to draw his readers to Christ. As Christ is above all other subjects, so Christ crucified is above all that can be said about Christ.

Third, the apostle mentions the manner of his preaching: "I was with you in weakness, and in fear, and in much trembling. And my speech and my preaching was not with enticing words of man's wisdom" (1 Cor. 2:3–4). Whenever he preached Christ crucified, he preached Him in a crucified style—plainly and diligently. His sermons were so full of Christ that his hearers might have concluded that he was acquainted with no other subject.

Doctrine: There is no truth more excellent in itself, or more necessary to be studied and preached, than the truth of Jesus Christ and Him crucified.

All other knowledge, no matter how much it is magnified in the world, is to be esteemed as rubbish in comparison to the excellence of the knowledge of Christ (Phil. 3:8; Col. 2:3). Its lovely properties render it superior to all other studies.

First, the knowledge of Christ is *central*. It is the scope and center of all divine revelation. The blessed lines of the Old and New Testaments meet in Christ. They harmonize and sweetly center in Him, as we see in the epistle to the Hebrews. The knowledge of Christ is a key that unlocks the greatest part of the sacred Scriptures. Like a clue, it leads us through the whole labyrinth of the Scriptures.

Second, the knowledge of Christ is *foundational*. (1) It is foundational to all graces. The opening of the eyes is the Holy Spirit's first work, and His subsequent work depends on an increase in knowledge (Col. 3:10; 2 Peter 3:18). Grace and knowledge keep equal pace in a believer's soul—as one increases, so too does the other. (2) It is foundational to all duties. Faith and hope are impossible without knowledge (Isa. 53:11; John 6:40; Col. 2:17; Heb. 6:19; 1 Peter 1:3). Prayer is also impossible without knowledge, for the true way of conversing with God is by believing in Him through a mediator. The knowledge of Christ, therefore, is indispensable to all who approach God in any duty. (3) It is foundational to all comforts. Christ is the object of our joy (Phil. 3:3). Without the knowledge of Him, we are the most miserable creatures in the world. But when He manifests Himself, shining the beams of His light into our souls, we sing in the midst of affliction and shout in the pains of death, as those who find great treasure. (4) It is foundational to eternal happiness. We cannot be saved without the knowledge of Christ. "And this is life eternal, that they might know thee the only true God, and Jesus Christ, whom thou hast sent" (John 17:3). If it is eternal life to know Christ, then it is eternal damnation to be ignorant of Him.

Third, the knowledge of Christ is *profound*. It is a boundless and bottomless ocean (Eph. 3:18). There is a "manifold wisdom of God" in Christ (Eph. 3:10). It is indeed pure, simple, and unmixed with anything but itself, yet it is manifold in kinds, degrees, and administrations. Something of Christ is revealed in one age, and something in another age, yet eternity itself cannot fully reveal Him.

Fourth, the knowledge of Christ is *honorable*. Those who devote themselves to other studies weary themselves at a children's game. The truths discovered in Christ are the very secrets that lay hidden in the bosom of God from all eternity (Eph. 3:8–9). God's heart is opened to us in Christ (John 1:18). This is why studying Christ in the gospel stamps a heavenly glory upon the soul (1 Cor. 3:9, 18).

Fifth, the knowledge of Christ is *comfortable*. When we study Him, we dig among the springs of comfort. The deeper we dig, the more these springs flow to us. Our hearts are ravished with the discoveries of Christ in the gospel. We could sit from morning to evening, listening to discourses about Christ, for "his mouth is most sweet" (Song 5:16).

Sixth, the knowledge of Christ is *incomparable*. When we compare it with all other knowledge, we further discover its excellence. (1) All other knowledge is natural, but this is supernatural. "No man knoweth the Son, but the Father; neither knoweth any man the Father, save the Son, and he to whomsoever the Son will reveal him" (Matt. 11:27). (2) All other knowledge depends on human intelligence, but this depends on the Holy Spirit. "I thank thee, O Father, Lord of heaven and earth, because thou hast hid these things from the wise and prudent, and hast revealed them unto babes" (Matt. 11:25; see also 1 Cor. 1:26–27). (3) All other knowledge fails to bring us to heaven, but this is a saving knowledge (1 Tim. 2:4). It has powerful influences whereby it transforms us into God's image (2 Cor. 3:18).

Application
Lesson 1
It informs us. The knowledge of Christ is sufficient to make us wise unto salvation. A little of this knowledge will do our souls more service than all the vain speculations in the world. We should not be discouraged when we see others far exceed us in other kinds of knowledge. If we know Christ, we know enough to save and comfort our souls. Many educated philosophers are in hell, while many illiterate Christians are in heaven.

Lesson 2
It humbles us. We know so little of Christ in comparison to what there is to know (1 Cor. 3:1–2; Heb. 5:12–14). How much time do we spend in vain discourses, frivolous pursuits, and worldly employments in comparison to the time we spend in the study of Christ?

Lesson 3
It challenges us. Many people content themselves with an impractical, ineffectual, and notional knowledge of Christ. The apostle declares, "It had been better for them not to

have known" (2 Peter 2:21). Notional knowledge only serves to aggravate sin and misery. It does not save anyone. It puts some weak restraints on people's sins, but their lusts eventually break down these restraints, thereby exposing them to greater damnation.

Lesson 4

It trains us. We see how we are to judge ministers. It is the highest commendation to be an able minister of Scripture, for here are all the treasures of knowledge. The best minister is able to display Christ in a lively and powerful manner before others, setting Him forth as crucified among them. The best sermon is full of Christ. Ministers should not be careless in language or method, but the excellency of a sermon lies not in these things but in the plainest discovery and liveliest application of Christ.

Lesson 5

It comforts us. Peace and comfort are found in the study of Christ and Him crucified. Why do we spend ourselves on other studies when all excellence and sweetness are concentrated in Christ? In all seasons and conditions, the fruits of comfort spring forth from the knowledge of Him (Rev. 22:2). O we must study Christ! We must study to know Him more *extensively*. There are many excellencies in Christ, which the most keen-sighted believer has not yet seen. And we must study to know Him more *intensively*. We need the lively power of this knowledge upon our hearts. This is the knowledge that carries all comfort and sweetness in it. We should devote our time and strength to this most sweet transcendent study.

Lesson 6

It warns us. First, ministers must take heed to their ministry. How? (1) They must set Christ before their people. It is the minister's calling to woo and win souls to Christ by presenting Him in all His excellence, so that hearts are ravished with His beauty and charmed into His arms. (2) They must make certain that their knowledge of Christ is not barren or powerless. As it passes from their minds to their lips, it ought to melt, sweeten, and ravish their hearts. A holy calling (without a holy heart) never saved anyone. O let the keepers of the vineyard keep their own vineyard! (3) They must not withhold the knowledge of Christ from their people. They must remember that the Great Shepherd gave Himself for the flock, and that He gave them to the flock; therefore, their time and gifts are not their own, but God's. Christ died for the sheep. Ministers, therefore, must watch, study, preach, pray, and do whatever they can for their salvation.

Second, we must not reject or despise the knowledge of Christ. (1) We despise the knowledge of Christ when we despise the means to that knowledge. If we reject knowledge, God will reject us for it. "He that heareth you heareth me; and he that despiseth you despiseth me; and he that despiseth me despiseth him that sent me" (Luke 10:16). (2) We despise the knowledge of Christ when we despise the directions and constraints of that knowledge. When we refuse to be guided by our knowledge, our light and our lusts struggle within us. It is sad when our lusts master our light. When we sin, we slight the warnings of our own consciences and offer violence to our own convictions.

Third, we must not satisfy ourselves in the knowledge that we have attained. We must press on to perfection. Upon acquiring a few notions of Christ, many professing believers swell with self-conceit. This is a grave sin, especially when we see how deep the knowledge of Christ lies and what pains we must take to dig for it. To throw away the shovel of duty and claim that we do not need to dig is presumption. We must not let our candle go out. We must devote ourselves to this study. Whatever communion God maintains with us, it is by means of the knowledge of Christ. Thus, we must count all things as trash in comparison to the excellence of this knowledge.

2

Christ's Essential Glory

Then was I by him, as one brought up with him: and I was daily his delight, rejoicing always before him.
—PROVERBS 8:30

This verse is part of a commendation of wisdom. "Wisdom is the principal thing" (Prov. 4:7). By *wisdom* Solomon means grace (or holiness) and Christ, who is the fountain of that grace. The first is famous for its excellence (Job 28:14–15), and so too is the second. In this verse, the Spirit of God describes the blessed state of Christ, the Wisdom of the Father, according to those eternal delights which He had with His Father before assuming our nature: "Then was I by him." These delights were twofold. (1) The Father and Son delighted in each other: "I was daily his delight, rejoicing always before him." (2) The Father and Son delighted in the prospect of the salvation of a people: "Rejoicing in the habitable part of his earth; and my delights were with the sons of men" (Prov. 8:31). My present business lies in the former—namely, the mutual delight of the Father and Son—and we must observe three things.

First, the glorious condition of the preincarnate Son of God is described according to His fellowship with His Father:

"Then was I by him." This means the Son was with the Father in a unique way. The "only begotten Son" was "in the bosom of the Father" (John 1:18). This is the greatest expression of nearness and intimacy. It is as if He should say that He was wrapped up in the very soul of His Father—embraced in God.

Second, this fellowship is illustrated by a metaphor: "as one brought up with him." Christ is here compared to a delightful child, playing before his father. The Hebrew root, which our translation renders "rejoicing always before him," means to laugh, play, or rejoice. As parents delight to see their children playing before them, so the Father delighted in beholding this darling of His heart.

Third, this delight is amplified by its permanence: "I was daily his delight, rejoicing always before him." This mutual delight was without a moment's interruption or diminution. These great and glorious persons let forth their fullest pleasure and delight into each other's heart. They lay (as it were) embraced in one another, entertaining themselves with ineffable and inconceivable delights and pleasures.

Doctrine: Christ's state before His incarnation was one of unspeakable delight and pleasure in the enjoyment of His Father.

The apostle John tells us that the Son was in the "bosom" of His Father (John 1:18). To lie in the bosom is a posture of dearest love (John 13:23). The Father describes His Son as "mine elect, in whom my soul delighteth" (Isa. 42:1). In this state, the Son is said to be "rich" (2 Cor. 8:9), "equal with God," and "in the form of God" (Phil. 2:6)—to have all the glory of the majesty of God. These riches were no less than all that God the Father has. "All things that the Father hath are mine" (John 16:15). What Christ now has in His exalted state is the same as what He had before His humiliation (John 17:5). I will describe the unspeakable felicity of Christ's state, while He lay in the "bosom" of His Father, in three ways.

Negatively

Let us consider Christ's state by removing all those degrees of abasement that His incarnation brought upon Him. First, in His preincarnate state, Christ was not a creature. It was at the incarnation that He "made himself of no reputation" (Phil. 2:7). This step of humiliation emptied Him of His glory. For God to be made man is such an abasement as no one can express. He not only appeared in true flesh but "in the likeness of sinful flesh" (Rom. 8:3).

Second, in His preincarnate state, Christ was not under the law. It was at the incarnation that "God sent forth his Son, made of a woman, made under the law" (Gal. 4:4). This was an inconceivable abasement to the absolute and independent Being. He not only came under the requirement of the law but under its curse.

Third, in His preincarnate state, Christ was not liable to a frail and feeble condition. (1) He knew nothing of grief. There was no sorrowing or sighing in the bosom where He lay. But, by the incarnation, He became "a man of sorrows" (Isa. 53:3). (2) He knew nothing of poverty. But by the incarnation, He had nowhere "to lay his head" (Matt. 8:20). (3) He knew nothing of reproach or shame. There was nothing but glory and honor reflected upon Him by His Father. But by the incarnation, He was "despised and rejected of men" (Isa.

53:3). (4) He knew nothing of temptation from the devil. He never knew what it was to be assaulted with temptations or to be assaulted by demons. But by the incarnation, He was "led up of the Spirit into the wilderness to be tempted of the devil" (Matt. 4:1). (5) He knew nothing of pain and torture in soul and body. But by the incarnation, He was "wounded" and "bruised" (Isa. 53:5). (6) He knew nothing of the hiding (or withdrawing) of His Father. There was never a cloud upon the face of God. But by the incarnation, He cried, "My God, my God, why hast thou forsaken me?" (Matt. 27:46). (7) He knew nothing of the impressions of His Father's wrath upon Him. But by the incarnation, He drank the bitter cup of God's judgment (Matt. 26:39).

All these things were new to Christ. He was above them all until He voluntarily subjected Himself to them for our sakes.

Positively

Let us consider Christ's preincarnate state according to what it was. First, it was a state of matchless happiness. He was with God (John 1:1), who is the fountain of all joy and delight (Ps. 16:11). To be wrapped up in the bosom of all delights must be a state that transcends comprehension. To have the fountain of love and delight communicating Himself so fully, immediately, and everlastingly upon the only begotten darling of His soul must be a state of transcendent felicity.

Second, it was a state of sweet communion. Christ was not only near and dear to God, but one with Him. "I and my Father are one" (John 10:30). They are one in nature, will, love, and delight. There is indeed a moral union of souls among people by love, but Christ's union with His Father was a natural oneness. No child is as one with his father, no husband is as one with his wife, no friend is as one with his friend, no soul is as one with its body as Christ and His Father were one. O what matchless delight must necessarily flow from such a blessed union!

Third, it was a state of pure delight. Our delight in one another is mixed. While there is something enjoyable, there is also something distasteful. The purer any delight is, the more excellent it is. There are no crystal streams flowing so purely from the fountain as the love and delight between these glorious persons. The Father embraced the Son with a most holy delight.

Fourth, it was a state of constant delight. It was "from everlasting" (Prov. 8:23). It never suffered a moment's interruption. The overflowing fountain of God's love and delight never stopped its course. "I was daily his delight, rejoicing always before him." The term in the original is plural ("delights"), pointing to its fullness.

Comparatively
Let us consider Christ's preincarnate state by comparing it with other delights. First, the delight that creatures take in one another is sometimes great. Jacob delighted in Benjamin so much that his life was "bound up" in his son's life (Gen. 44:30). Jonathan delighted in David and "loved him as his own soul" (1 Sam. 18:1). Yet this delight is finite, according to the measure and ability of creatures. In comparison, the delight between the Father and the Son is infinite, suitable to the infinite perfection of the divine being.

Second, the delight that God takes in the creature is sometimes great. He takes pleasure in His saints and rejoices "over [them] with singing" (Zeph. 3:17). Yet there is a great difference between His delight in creatures and His delight in Christ. All His delight in the saints is secondary and for Christ's sake, but His delight in Christ is primary and for His own sake. We are accepted in the Beloved (Eph. 1:6), whereas Christ is loved and accepted for Himself.

Third, the delight that creatures take in God and Christ is great. It is indeed a choice delight and transcendent love (Ps. 73:25). But, surely, our delight in God is no rule by which to measure the Father's delight in Christ. Our love to God (at the best) is still imperfect, but His love for Christ is perfect. Our love is variable, ebbing and flowing, but His love is constant.

In conclusion, Christ's condition and state before His incarnation was a state of matchless delight in the enjoyment of His Father.

Application

Lesson 1

The Father's love for poor sinners is astonishing. "God so loved the world, that he gave his only begotten Son" (John 3:16). Who among us would deliver the child of our delight to death, for the greatest inheritance in the world? The death of a child makes a great hole in a parent's heart. It is never closed in this world. No child ever lay so close to a parent's heart as Christ did to His Father's. And yet the Father willingly parts with His only Son—and that to a cursed death for the worst of sinners. O the admirable love of God! If the Father had not loved us, He would never have parted with such a Son for us. We must, therefore, give equal glory to the Father with the Son (John 5:23).

Lesson 2

Christ's love for poor sinners is astonishing. He consented to leave such a bosom, and the ineffable delights that were there, for such poor worms as us. O the height, depth, length, and breadth of immeasurable love! Christ's love is commended to poor sinners. He was embraced in the Father's bosom in a manner unknown to us, yet He freely laid down its glory and riches for our sakes (Rom. 5:6–8). As the Father loved Him, even so He has loved us (John 17:23). What manner of love is this! Who has ever loved as Christ loves? Who has ever denied himself for Christ as Christ has denied Himself for us?

Lesson 3

Interest in Christ is the true way to all spiritual preferment in heaven. Do we desire to be in favor with God? We must get an interest in Christ. We are received and welcomed by God according to our interest in the Beloved (Eph. 1:6). Because Christ is the great favorite in heaven, His image upon our souls and His name in our prayers make both accepted with God.

Lesson 4

Christ is worthy of our love and delight. He ravishes God's heart, and will He not ravish our hearts? Surely, He alone is worthy of our precious affections. May the Lord direct our hearts into the love of Christ! Our hearts, love, and delight ought to meet with the heart of God in this most blessed object. He who left God's bosom for us ought to be embraced by us.

Lesson 5

It grieves the heart of God to see sinners despise and reject His dear Son. Unbelievers trample upon God's darling, and they tread underfoot the One who lay eternally in His bosom (Heb. 10:29). They smite the apple of God's eye. How will God respond to this? Surely, He will destroy such wretched sinners (Matt. 21:37–40). Sinners will one day know the price of this sin. They will feel what it is to despise Christ, who is able to compel love from the hardest heart. O that sinners would slight Him no more! O that this day their hearts might fall in love with Him! No matter what guilt or discouragement we experience, we can embrace Christ, who is freely offered to us. When we do, we are as dear to God as the most eminent believer in the world. But God's wrath is treasured up for those who continue to neglect such a savior (Heb. 10:26–28).

Lesson 6

Christ lay eternally in this bosom of love, and yet He was content to leave it for our sakes. Therefore, we must (1) be ready to leave all earthly comforts for Christ (Luke 18:26–28), (2) be confident in prayer that we are heard and accepted through the Beloved (John 11:42; Eph. 1:6; Heb. 7:25), and (3) be patient in death as we are going to that bosom of love from which Christ came (John 17:5, 24). This should be a great encouragement to us. We can comfort one another with these words: "I am leaving the bosom of a creature, and I am going to the bosom of God."

3

The Covenant of Redemption

Therefore will I divide him a portion with the great, and he shall divide the spoil with the strong; because he hath poured out his soul unto death: and he was numbered with the transgressors; and he bare the sin of many, and made intercession for the transgressors.

—ISAIAH 53:12

The subject of Isaiah 53 is Christ's death and its glorious result. Though He suffered grievously, it was not for His own sins: "he had done no violence, neither was any deceit in his mouth" (v. 9). Rather, He suffered in His capacity as a surety for us: "The LORD hath laid on him the iniquity of us all" (v. 6). It is plainly asserted that He came to stand in this capacity by compact and agreement with His Father before the world was made (vv. 10–12). In our verse, we see two things.

First, Christ's *work*: "he bare the sin of many, and made intercession for the transgressors." It was indeed a hard work for Him to pour out His soul unto death. It was aggravated by His companions, in that "he was numbered with the transgressors."

Second, Christ's *reward*: "Therefore will I divide him a portion with the great, and he shall divide the spoil with the strong." This is an allusion to conquerors in war, for whom are reserved the richest garments and most honorable captives (Isa. 45:14).

Some say Christ's work has no other relation to His reward than that of an antecedent to a consequent. Others say His work is a meritorious cause of His reward. I do not see any absurdity in calling Christ's exaltation the reward and fruit of His humiliation. The Father here promises to give Him this reward if He will undertake the redemption of the elect by pouring out His soul unto death.

Doctrine: The business of man's salvation was transacted upon covenant terms between the Father and the Son in all eternity.

This covenant of redemption differs from the covenant of grace in several ways. (1) They differ in their *persons*. In the covenant of redemption, it is the Father and the Son who mutually covenant, whereas in the covenant of grace, it is God and us. (2) They differ in their *precepts*. The covenant of redemption requires Christ to shed His blood, whereas the covenant of grace requires us to believe. (3) They differ in their *promises*. In the covenant of redemption, God promises to Christ a name above every name and dominion from sea to sea, whereas in the covenant of grace, He promises to us grace and glory. These are two distinct covenants.

The substance of the covenant of redemption is expressed in Isaiah 49, where Christ begins by revealing His commission, explaining how His Father had called Him and prepared

Him for the work of redemption (vv. 1–2). The Father then offers to Christ the elect of Israel for His reward (v. 3). But Christ is not satisfied with these, and therefore He complains, "I have laboured in vain, I have spent my strength for nought" (v. 4). This is but a small reward for so great a suffering as He must undergo. His blood is worth much more than this. It is sufficient to redeem all the elect dispersed among the Gentiles as well as the lost sheep of the house of Israel. The Father responds by telling Him that He intends to reward Him better than this: "It is a light thing that thou shouldest be my servant to raise up the tribes of Jacob, and to restore the preserved of Israel: I will also give thee for a light to the Gentiles, that thou mayest be my salvation unto the end of the earth" (v. 6). Thus, the covenant is carried on between them, transacting it after the manner of men. For the better understanding of this covenant, I will consider six points.

The Persons
The persons transacting with each other in this covenant are God the Father and God the Son. The first functions as a creditor and the second as a surety. The Father requires satisfaction, while the Son engages to give it. Christ is the natural Son of God and therefore most fit to make us the adopted sons of God.

The Business
The business transacted between the Father and the Son was the redemption of all God's elect. Our eternal happiness was before them, and our everlasting concerns were in their hands. The elect (not yet in existence) are here considered as existing

and as fallen and miserable creatures. The business before the Father and the Son is how we may be restored to happiness without prejudice to God's honor, justice, and truth.

The Manner

The manner of the transaction was federal (or covenantal). In other words, it was by mutual engagements and stipulations, each person undertaking to perform His part in order to secure our recovery. The Father promises to hold His Son's hand and keep Him (Isa. 42:6). The Son promises to obey His Father's call to suffer (Isa. 50:5). Having made these promises, each holds the other to His engagement. The Father requires the satisfaction that was promised to Him. When Christ is making the payment, the Father does not abate anything of the full price: God "spared not his own Son" (Rom. 8:32). As the Father stood strictly upon the terms of the covenant, so did Christ: "I have glorified thee on the earth: I have finished the work which thou gavest me to do. And now, O Father, glorify thou me with thine own self" (John 17:4–5). It is as if He had said, "Father, the work is done. Now where are the wages I was promised?"

The Articles

Here we will consider the articles (or promises) to which they both agree. The Father promises to do five things for Christ.

First, He promises to invest Him and anoint Him to a threefold office, answerable to the misery that lay upon the elect. The guilt of our sin must be expiated, our blindness of mind must be cured, and our bondage to sin must be broken. Therefore, God must make Christ unto us "wisdom, and righteousness, and sanctification, and redemption" (1 Cor. 1:30). He is made so to us as our prophet, priest, and king. Christ could not put Himself into any of these offices without a commission to act authoritatively. For this reason, the Father promises to seal Him with a threefold commission: He promises to invest Him with an eternal and royal priesthood (Ps. 110:4; Heb. 7:16–17, 24–25); He promises to make Him a prophet (Isa. 42:6–7); and He promises to make Him a king of the whole empire of the world (Ps. 2:6–8). Thus, the Father promises to qualify and furnish Christ completely for the work of redemption by His investiture with this threefold office.

Second, the Father promises to stand by Christ and assist and strengthen Him for His difficult work (Isa. 42:5–7). He promises to support His humanity when it is weighed down with the burden that was to come upon it (Mark 14:34). Indeed, Christ's humanity needed a support of no less strength than the infinite power of the Godhead.

Third, the Father promises to crown Christ's work with success (Isa. 53:10). Christ will not shed His invaluable blood upon hazardous terms, but He will see and reap its sweet fruits.

Fourth, the Father promises to accept Christ in His work. "Yet shall I be glorious in the eyes of the LORD" (Isa. 49:5). Here Christ expresses His faith in His Father's promise. Accordingly, the Father manifests His satisfaction in Him and His work. While Christ was on the earth, there came a voice from heaven, saying, "This is my beloved Son, in whom I am well pleased" (Matt. 3:17; 17:5).

Fifth, the Father promises to reward Christ for His work by exalting Him to supreme glory and honor. "I will declare the decree: the LORD hath said unto me, Thou art my Son;

this day have I begotten thee" (Ps. 2:7). These words are spoken of the day of His resurrection, when He finished His suffering (Acts 13:32–33). At that time, the Father wiped away the reproach of His cross and invested Him with such glory that He looked like Himself again.

These are the encouragements that the Father proposed and promised to His Son. This was the "joy that was set before him" whereby Christ so patiently "endured the cross, despising the shame" (Heb. 12:2).

In like manner, Christ gives His engagement to the Father. He is content to be made flesh, to divest Himself of His glory, to come under the obedience and malediction of the law, and to submit to the hardest sufferings it should please His Father to inflict on Him (Isa. 50:5–7). When He says, "I was not rebellious," He means that He was heartily willing and content to accept the terms. The sense of this place is well delivered to us in Psalm 40:6–10.

The Performance

Having consented, the Son applied Himself to the discharge of His work. He took a body, fulfilled all righteousness (Matt. 3:15), and made His soul an offering for sin. As a result, He could say, "I have glorified thee on the earth: I have finished the work which thou gavest me to do" (John 17:4). Christ went through all the parts of His active and passive obedience cheerfully and faithfully. The Father made good His engagements to Christ with no less faithfulness. He promised to assist Him and support Him, and so He did (Luke 22:43). He promised to accept Him in His work (that He should be glorious in His eyes), and so He did (Luke 3:22). He promised Him that "he should see his seed," and so He did, for ever since then His blood has been fruitful in the world. He promised to reward Him and exalt Him, and so He did (Phil. 2:9–11).

The Timing
This compact between the Father and the Son was made in eternity. Before He made the world, His delight was in Him. When we had no existence (except in the infinite mind and purpose of God), He gave us this grace of redemption in Christ (2 Tim. 1:9).

Application
Lesson 1
It offers abundant assurance of our salvation. God made the covenant of redemption with Christ for us, and it is the foundation of the covenant of grace. God's promise is security enough for our faith, but His covenant of grace adds an additional security. When we look at the covenant of grace, we do not question God's performance, but we often stumble at the great defects in our performance. But when we look at the covenant of redemption, there is nothing to stagger our faith. Both of the persons involved (the Father and the Son) are infinitely able and faithful to perform their parts. There is no possibility of failure. When puzzled and perplexed, we turn our eyes away from the defects in our obedience to the fullness and completeness of Christ's obedience. We see ourselves complete in Him, when most defective in ourselves.

Lesson 2
It informs us that the Father and the Son mutually rely upon one another in the business of our redemption. The Father

relies upon the Son for the performance of His part (Isa. 42:1). The Father so trusted Christ that, upon the credit of His promise to come into the world and to become a sacrifice for the elect, He saved all the Old Testament saints (Heb. 11:39–40). As the Father relied upon and trusted Christ, so Christ relied upon and trusted His Father. Having performed His part and departed the world, He now trusts His Father for the accomplishment of His promise: "he shall see his seed" (Isa. 53:10). He depends upon His Father for all the elect, that He will preserve them unto the heavenly kingdom (John 17:11).

Lesson 3

It infers the unquestionable success of Christ's intercession in heaven for believers. "He ever liveth to make intercession for them" (Heb. 7:25). His blood "speaketh better things" for them (Heb. 12:24). Because of the covenant of redemption, it is certain that Christ's blood will obtain that for which it pleads in heaven. What He now asks of His Father is the very thing that His Father promised Him before the world began. Whatever He asks for us is as due to Him as the wages of the laborer when his work is done. If the work is done, and done faithfully, as the Father has acknowledged it is, then the reward is due immediately. There is no doubt that He will receive it from the hands of a righteous God.

Lesson 4

It instructs us as to the consistency of grace with full satisfaction to the justice of God. We are saved "according to his own purpose and grace, which was given us in Christ Jesus before the world began" (2 Tim. 1:9). That is to say, it was given to us according to the gracious terms of the covenant of redemption. However, God still requires satisfaction from Christ. Grace to us and satisfaction to God's justice are not inconsistent. What was a debt to Christ is grace to us. "Being justified freely by his grace through the redemption that is in Christ" (Rom. 3:24).

Lesson 5

It informs us of the antiquity of God's love for believers. He loved us, provided for us, and contrived all our happiness before we existed. We reap the fruit of this covenant in the present, but its seed was sown from eternity. It is not only ancient but free, for there was nothing in us to engage God's love because we did not yet exist.

Lesson 6

It informs us that it is reasonable for believers to embrace the hardest terms of obedience to Christ. He complied with such hard terms for our salvation. If He had not poured out His soul to death, He would not have enjoyed one of us. When they struck this bargain, we can imagine them saying:

> Father: *My Son, here are poor miserable souls who have utterly undone themselves, and now lie open to My justice. Justice demands satisfaction for them, or else it will satisfy itself in their eternal ruin. What will be done for these souls?*
>
> Son: *O My Father, such is My love and pity for them that I will be responsible for them as their surety. Show Me what they owe You. You may require it at My hand. I choose to suffer Your wrath rather than see them suffer it. Father, may all their debt be upon Me!*

Father: *But, My Son, if You undertake this for them, You must pay every debt. There will be no abatements. If I spare them, I will not spare You.*

Son: *Father, let it be so. Charge it all to Me! I am able to discharge it. Although it impoverishes all My riches and empties all My treasures (2 Cor. 8:9), I am content to do it.*

O how can we shrink at a few petty difficulties, and complain that it is too hard and harsh for us? If we knew the grace of our Lord Jesus Christ in His wonderful condescension for us, we could not do it.

Lesson 7

It infers that we should make certain that we are among the number which the Father and the Son agreed to save, that we were comprehended in Christ's engagement and compact with the Father. We may know this without ascending into heaven or prying into unrevealed secrets, for all whom the Father gave to Christ believe that the Father sent Christ (John 17:8). We know God in Christ (John 17:6, 25). We belong to another world (John 17:16; Gal. 6:14; Heb. 11:13–14). We keep His Word (John 17:6); that is to say, we receive its sanctifying effects and influences into our hearts whereby we persevere in the profession and practice of it to the end (John 17:17). These are the persons whom the Father delivered to Christ, and He accepted from the Father, in this blessed covenant.

4

God's Admirable Love

For God so loved the world, that
he gave his only begotten Son.
—JOHN 3:16

We have heard of God's gracious design to recover poor sinners to Himself through Christ and how this design was contrived in the covenant of redemption. Now we will hear, from this verse, how His design was advanced by one degree toward its accomplishment in His giving His Son for us: "God so loved the world, that he gave his only begotten Son."

The preceding verses reveal the nature and necessity of regeneration. This verse infers its necessity from the peculiar respect that God has upon believers in giving Christ for them. They alone reap all the special and saving benefits and advantages of that gift: "God so loved the world, that he gave his only begotten Son, that whosoever believeth in him should not perish." There are four points to consider.

First, the original fountain of our mercies is God's love. (1) His *benevolent* love is His desire and purpose to save and do good. Thus, His gracious purpose to Jacob is called "love"

(Rom. 9:13). (2) His *beneficent* love is His actual doing good to those whom He loves. It is His bestowing the effects of His love upon us. (3) His *complacent* love is His delight and satisfaction in beholding the fruit of the grace that He first intended for us (benevolent love) and then actually bestowed on us (beneficent love). God's benevolent love was handled in the previous sermon—namely, God's design to save us according to the terms and articles of His compact with Christ. God's beneficent love is in view in our verse. Out of the fountain of God's benevolent love flowed His beneficent love (Christ) to us. Both lead to His complacent love, for He both purposed and bestowed Christ on us so that He might everlastingly delight in beholding the glory and praise of all this reflected on Himself by His redeemed ones. This, then, is the fountain of our mercies.

Second, the mercy flowing out of this fountain is Christ (Luke 1:72). He is the marrow, kernel, and substance of all other mercies. This love is expressed with a double emphasis in our verse. The first is the particle *so*. How did God love the world? He *so* loved it. The second emphasis is the expression *only begotten Son*. To have given a son would have been wonderful, but to give His only begotten Son is inexpressible love.

Third, the object of God's love is the world. This respects God's elect in the world—that is, those who do (or will) believe. The term *world* is used to signify the elect because they are scattered throughout all parts and among all ranks of people. These are the objects of God's love. It is not angels but people who were so loved. He is called a Lover or Friend of people, but never the Lover or Friend of angels or creatures.

Fourth, this mercy flows to us freely and spontaneously.

He "gave" His Son. Moreover, Christ freely gave Himself (Gal. 2:20). The Father gave Christ out of good will to us, and Christ as willingly gave Himself.

Doctrine: The gift of Christ is the highest and fullest manifestation of God's love for sinners that was ever made.

"Herein is love, not that we loved God, but that he loved us, and sent his Son to be the propitiation for our sins" (1 John 4:10). Why does the apostle magnify this gift by saying, "Herein is love," as if there were love in nothing else? Do we not see God's love in His provision and protection? Yes, but there is no love in these things as compared to the love expressed in giving Christ for us. These are great mercies, but when compared to this mercy, they are like the light of candles when brought into the sunshine. It is remarkable that when the apostle declares the fruit that most commends God's love for us, he says, "But God commendeth his love toward us, in that, while we were yet sinners, Christ died for us" (Rom. 5:8). This is the very flower of His love.

The Nature of God's Gift

How was Christ given by the Father? We must not think that God parted with His interest in His Son. When people give, they transfer property to another. But when God gave Christ, He was still as much His as ever. His giving of Christ implies the following. First, He appointed Christ unto death for us (Acts 2:23). By the counsel and purpose of God, Christ was chosen and set apart for His service (Isa. 42:1). Second, He parted with Christ for a time. There was a kind of parting between the Father and the Son when He came to tabernacle in our flesh (John 16:28). The distance established by His incarnation and humiliation was proper to His humanity, which was really distant from God's glory. Third, He delivered Christ into the hands of justice to be punished (Acts 2:23; Rom. 8:32). Fourth, He applied Christ (with all that He purchased by His blood) to us as a portion and inheritance (John 4:10; 6:32–33).

The Value of God's Gift

How was God's gift of Christ the highest and fullest manifestation of His love that the world has ever seen? First, we must consider how near and dear Christ was to the Father. He was His only Son, the Son of His love, the darling of His soul, the express image of His person, the brightness of His glory. In parting with Christ, He parted with "his dear Son" (Col. 1:13). Our dearest children are but strangers to us in comparison to the unspeakable nearness that was between the Father and Christ. His willingness to part with His Son is a manifestation of a love that we will admire for all eternity.

Second, we must consider the reason the Father gave Christ—namely, to die on the cross, to be made a curse, to be scorned and ridiculed, to endure unparalleled sufferings. It breaks our hearts to see our children striving in the pangs of death. But the Father beheld His Son struggling under agonies that no one has ever felt. He saw Him falling to the ground, groveling in the dust, and sweating blood. He heard His heartrending cry: "Father, if thou be willing, remove this cup from me" (Luke 22:42). Christ was delivered to the wrath of an infinite God, to the very torments of hell, and that by the hand of His own Father.

Third, we must consider that, in giving Christ, the Father

gave the richest jewel in His treasure—a mercy of great worth and inestimable value. God bestowed the mercy of mercies, the most precious thing in heaven and earth, upon poor sinners. As great, lovely, and excellent as His Son was, He did not account Him too good to bestow upon us. O what manner of love is this!

Fourth, we must consider on whom the Father bestowed His Son. Upon friends? No. Upon enemies (Rom. 5:8–10). Who would part with a son for the sake of enemies? O unspeakable love!

Fifth, we must consider how freely this gift came from the Father. It was not forced out of His hand, for we neither desired nor deserved it. It was eternal love that delivered Him to us (1 John 4:19).

Application
Lesson 1
Souls are exceedingly precious. God gives His only Son out of His bosom as a ransom for us. Surely, this speaks of our value in His sight. God would not have parted with such a Son for small matters. "Ye were not redeemed with corruptible things, as silver and gold…but with the precious blood of Christ" (1 Peter 1:18–19). God had such esteem for us that Christ was made a curse for us. O we must learn to put a due value upon our own souls. We must remember what a treasure we carry with us. The glory that we see in this world is not equivalent to the soul's worth (Matt. 16:26).

Lesson 2
We may rightly expect all temporal mercies from Him (Rom. 8:32; 1 Cor. 3:21–22). We hold all other things in Christ,

who is the capital and most comprehensive mercy. These four things must be weighed and pondered in our thoughts. First, no other mercy is (or can be) so dear to God as Christ is. He never laid anything else in His bosom as He did His Son. There is no outward enjoyment that compares to Christ in God's estimation. If God has parted so freely with that which was infinitely dear to Him, how can He deny outward comforts when they may promote His glory and our good? Second, no other mercy is as great and excellent as Christ is. These things are but poor creatures, but He "is over all, God blessed for ever" (Rom. 9:5). They are common gifts, but He is the gift of God (John 4:10). They are ordinary mercies, but He is the mercy of God (Luke 1:72). If God has so freely given the greatest mercy, how can we suppose that He will deny lesser mercies? Third, we are entitled to all temporal mercies by the gift of Christ. As to right, they are conveyed to us with Christ (1 Cor. 3:21–23; 2 Cor. 1:20). With Christ, God has given us all things to enjoy (1 Tim. 6:17). Thus, we have all mercies upon account of our title to them in Christ. Fourth, God has given us this all-comprehending mercy when we were enemies to Him and alienated from Him; thus, it is unimaginable that He will deny us any inferior mercy when we have entered a state of reconciliation with Him (Rom. 5:8–10).

Lesson 3
The greatest evil is manifested in despising, slighting, and rejecting Christ. It is sad to abuse the love of God manifested in the lowest gift of providence, but to slight the richest discoveries of it in the Father's gift of His Son is astonishing. There is no guilt like this.

5

Christ's Wonderful Person

And the Word was made flesh, and dwelt among us.
—JOHN 1:14

The work propounded by the Father in the covenant of redemption infinitely exceeds the power of any mere creature to perform. He who undertakes to satisfy God by obedience must be God, and He who performs such perfect obedience in our place (by doing and suffering all that the law requires) must be man. These two natures must be united in one person, or else there could not be a cooperation of either nature in His mediatory work. How these natures are united in the wonderful person of our Immanuel is the first part of the great mystery of godliness, and it is declared in our verse: "And the Word was made flesh, and dwelt among us." Here the incarnation of the Son is plainly asserted. This assertion contains three parts.

First, the *person*: "the Word." He is the second person (or subsistent) in the most glorious Godhead. He is called "the Word" because He is the scope of the prophetic Word or because He reveals the mind and will of God to us: "The only begotten Son, which is in the bosom of the Father, he hath declared him" (John 1:18).

Second, the *nature*: "flesh." This is the entire human nature, consisting of a true human soul and body.

Third, the *assumption*: "the Word was made flesh." He took (or assumed) the true human nature (called "flesh") into the unity of His divine person, with all its integral parts and essential properties. And so, He "was made" (or became) a true and real man (Heb. 2:16). It was the work of the whole Trinity: God the Father in the Son by the Spirit formed (or created) that nature, yet it was the Son alone who was made flesh. We must not misconceive this to mean that there was a mutation of the Godhead into flesh, for the incarnation was performed "not by changing what He was, but by assuming what He was not" (Augustine). When Scripture says that Christ was "made…sin" (2 Cor. 5:21) or "made a curse" (Gal. 3:13), it does not mean that He was turned into sin or into a curse. Similarly, when we say that the Son became flesh, we must not think that the Godhead was turned into flesh and thereby lost its own being and nature.

This assertion ("the Word was made flesh") is strongly confirmed by the apostle John: "the Word was made flesh, and dwelt among us, (and we beheld his glory)." This was no illusion, but a most real and undeniable thing, for the apostles were eyewitnesses of it (1 John 1:1–3).

Doctrine: Christ really assumed the true and perfect human nature into a personal union with His divine nature, and He remains true God and true man in one person forever.

This doctrine declares one of the deepest mysteries of godliness (1 Tim. 3:16). It is a mystery by which apprehension is dazzled, invention is astonished, and all expression is swallowed. We walk here upon the brink of danger, for the slightest misstep might engulf us in the bogs of error. It is a doctrine hard to understand and dangerous to mistake. The Son assumed a true human body (Phil. 2:7–8; Heb. 2:14–16), and He assumed a true human soul (Matt. 26:38; 27:50). Both His natures (divine and human) make but one person (Rom. 1:3–4; 9:5). That we may have a sound and clear understanding of this mystery, I will consider the nature, effect, and purpose of this wonderful union.

The Nature of This Union
There are three dazzling unions in Scripture: (1) three persons in one God, *essentially*; (2) two distinct persons by one Spirit, *mystically*; and (3) two distinct natures in one person, *hypostatically*. My task is to explain the third.

First, we must not think that when Christ assumed our nature, it was united consubstantially as the three persons in the Godhead are united among themselves. They have but one and the same nature and will, but Christ (though He is one person) has two distinct natures and wills.

Second, we must not think that Christ's divine nature and human nature are united physically like the soul and body are united in one person. Death dissolves the union between soul and body. But the union between Christ's two natures is indissoluble. When His soul expired and His body was interred, both His soul and body were still united to the second person.

Third, we must not think that Christ's divine nature and human nature are united mystically like the union that is between Christ and believers. Though believers are said to be in Christ and Christ in them, they are not one person with Him.

The hypostatical union is that whereby the second person in the Godhead took the human nature into a personal union with Himself by virtue whereof the manhood subsists in the second person, yet without confusion, both making but one person, Immanuel (God with us). Though we ascribe a twofold nature to Christ, we do not ascribe a double person. The human nature of Christ never subsisted separately and distinctly by any personal subsistence of its own. From the first moment of conception, it subsisted in union with the second person. To explain this mystery more particularly, consider the following five points.

First, the human nature was united to the second person miraculously and extraordinarily, being supernaturally framed in the womb of the Virgin by the overshadowing power of the Most High (Luke 1:34–35). For this reason, it may truly and properly be said to be the fruit of the womb, but not by the loins of a man. This was necessary in order to exempt the assumed human nature from the pollution of Adam's sin. Christ received the human nature, not (as all others do) in the way of ordinary generation in which original sin is propagated. His human nature was extraordinarily produced and was a most pure and holy thing (Luke 1:35). The two natures could not be conjoined in the person of Christ if there had been the least taint of sin upon the human nature.

For God can have no fellowship with sin, much less be united to it (Heb. 7:26).

Second, the human nature was assumed integrally; that is to say, Christ took a complete and perfect human soul and body with every faculty and member. This was necessary so that He might heal the whole nature of the leprosy of sin which has seized and infected every member and faculty. He assumed all to sanctify all.

Third, the human nature was assumed with all its sinless infirmities (Heb. 2:17). These include hunger, thirst, weariness, sweating, bleeding, mortality, and so on. They are not in themselves formally and intrinsically sinful, yet they are the effects and consequents of sin. On that account, Christ is said to be sent "in the likeness of sinful flesh" (Rom. 8:3). Here we see the gracious condescension of Christ for us. He did not assume our innocent nature as it was in Adam before the fall while it stood in all its primitive glory and perfection, but He assumed it after sin had defaced, ruined, and spoiled it.

Fourth, the human nature is so united with the divine nature that each nature still retains its own essential properties. This distinction is not lost by the union. The divine and human are not confounded, but a line of distinction runs between them in this wonderful person.

Fifth, the union of the two natures in Christ is inseparable. The natural union between His soul and body was dissolved for a time by His death, but the hypostatical union remained as entire and firm as ever. Though His soul and body were divided from each other, yet neither of them was divided from the divine nature. When Christ died, His soul and body retained their union with the divine nature, though not (during that space) with each other.

And thus we are to form and regulate our conceptions of this great mystery.

The Effect of This Union

There are three immediate results of this marvelous union. First, the two natures are united in the person of the Mediator, and the properties of each nature are attributed (and do truly agree) in the whole person. Thus, it is proper to say that the Lord of glory was crucified (1 Cor. 2:8), that the blood of God redeemed the church (Acts 20:28), and that Christ was both in heaven and earth at the same time (John 3:13). Yet we do not believe that one nature imparts its properties to the other; that it is proper to say that the divine nature suffered, bled, or died; or that the human nature is omniscient, omnipotent, or omnipresent. The properties of both natures are so ascribed to the person that it is proper to affirm any of them of Him in the concrete, though not abstractly. The right understanding of this greatly assists in teaching the true sense of many dark passages of Scripture.

Second, another fruit of this hypostatical union is the singular advancement of the human nature in Christ far beyond what is possible in any other person. It is filled with an unparalleled measure of divine graces and excellencies (Ps. 8:4–6) and therefore becomes the object of adoration (Acts 7:59).

Third, Christ acts according to both natures in His mediatory work. The human nature does what is human (e.g., suffering, sweating, bleeding, dying), and His divine nature stamps all these with infinite value. And so, they sweetly concur unto one glorious work and design of mediation.

The Purpose of This Union
The last thing to be considered is the grounds and reasons of this assumption. The divine nature did not assume the human nature necessarily but voluntarily; that is to say, the divine nature did not assume the human nature to be perfected by it, but to prepare and qualify Christ for a full discharge of His mediatorship in the offices of prophet, priest, and king. (1) Without this double nature in the unity of His person, Christ could not have been our prophet. As God, He knows God's mind and will (John 1:18). As man, He is fitted to impart this knowledge to us (Deut. 18:15–18; Acts 20:22). (2) Without this double nature in the unity of His person, Christ could not have been our priest. If He had not been man, He could not have shed His blood. If He had not been God, His shed blood would not have been of adequate value for us (Acts 20:28). (3) Without this double nature in the unity of His person, Christ could not have been our king. If He had not been man, He would not have been related to us, and thus He would not have been a fit head for us. If He had not been God, He could neither rule nor defend His body, the church.

Application
Lesson 1
It is important to be convinced of this truth and to defend it against all adversaries. The dividing of Christ's person (which is one) and the confounding of His natures (which are two)

has been the occasion of those errors that have greatly disturbed the peace of the church. The Arians denied His deity. The Apollinarians maimed His humanity. The Sabellians affirmed that the Father and the Spirit were incarnated as well as the Son. Because of that absurdity, they were forced to deny the three distinct persons in the Godhead and affirm that they are but three names. The Eutychians confounded both natures in Christ, denying any distinction between them. The Seleusians affirmed that Christ unclothed Himself of His humanity when He ascended, and that He has no human body in heaven. The Nestorians so separate the two natures of Christ as to make them two distinct persons.

But we have not learned Christ in this way. We know that (1) He is true and very God; (2) He is true and very man; (3) the two natures make but one person, being united inseparably; and (4) the two natures are not confounded or swallowed up in one another, but remain distinct in the person of Christ. Great things hang upon all these truths. We must not remove a single stone from this foundation.

Lesson 2
It reveals the love of the Father and the Son. The Father so fervently willed our salvation that He was content to degrade the darling of His soul to so vile and contemptible a state (Phil. 2:7). He seems (as it were) to forget His relation to His own Son. "God so loved the world, that he gave his only begotten Son" (John 3:16). And how astonishing is the love of Christ that He would humble Himself to exalt us? It is ravishing to think that He would pass by a more excellent species of creatures, refusing the angelic nature, to take the human

nature (Heb. 2:16)—to make Himself a subject capable of sorrows, wounds, and tears. O that we would get our hearts suitably affected with these high impressions of the love of the Father and the Son!

Lesson 3
It reveals the infinite wisdom of God in devising the method of our recovery. Christ is indeed "the power…and the wisdom of God" (1 Cor. 1:24). The divine wisdom is more glorified in Him than in all of God's other works.

Lesson 4
The Christian religion is incomparably sweet, for it shows poor sinners a just foundation upon which to rest their trembling consciences. Formerly, our conscience saw God arming Himself with wrath to avenge; but now we see God coming down and so intimately uniting our flesh to Himself that it has no subsistence of its own but is united with the divine person. Hence, it is easy to imagine what value must be in that blood, and how eternal love flourishes into pardon, grace, and peace. Here is the way in which the sinner may see justice and mercy kissing each other. O happy are those who have dropped their anchor on this ground! They have peace.

Lesson 5
It is necessary that Christ should have a union with our particular persons as well as with our common nature. This union with our nature is utterly useless to us, and will do us no good, except He has a union with our person by faith. It is indeed infinite mercy that God has come so near to us as to dwell in our flesh, and that He has established such an excellent

method to save poor sinners. Do we refuse Him and shut our hearts against Him? If so, our sin is hereby aggravated beyond the sin of demons who never sinned against a mediator in their own nature. I doubt not that the demons will mock, for all eternity, those who have rejected such a great salvation.

Lesson 6

Christ is sensibly touched with the infirmities that attend human nature. This means He has pity and compassion for us under all our burdens (Heb. 2:17–18). O what a comfort is this! Our High Priest in heaven has our nature to enable Him to take compassion on us.

Lesson 7

God has laid the foundation of our eternal happiness in the incarnation of His Son. The glory of our body and soul is founded in Christ's taking our flesh upon Himself. God will transform our vile bodies and make them conformable to Christ's glorious body (Phil. 3:21). A greater honor cannot be done to human nature than what is already done by this grace of union, and our persons are incapable of a higher glory than what consists in our conformity to our glorious head, Christ. The flesh of Christ will always have a glory distinct from ours in heaven. It is advanced above our flesh and blood in two ways. First, subjectively, it is the flesh and blood of God (Acts 20:28), and so it has a distinct and incommunicable glory of its own. Second, objectively, it is the flesh and blood that all the angels and saints adore.

Lesson 8

It is a comfort to know that He who dwells in our flesh is God. A poor believer can take great joy from this. We are sure our beloved is Christ, and Christ is God. When we say, "Our Christ is God," we have said everything. We can say no more. He is God and man in one person. As man, He is full of an experimental sense of our wants, burdens, and infirmities. As God, He can support and supply them all.

6

The Authority of the Mediator

For him hath God the Father sealed.
—JOHN 6:27

We have heard of Christ's compact (or agreement) with the Father in the covenant of redemption, and we have heard of what the Father did in giving His Son out of His bosom and of what the Son did in assuming human nature. Everything He did in that assumed body would have been invalid without a due call and commission from His Father. This is what we have in this verse: "For him hath God the Father sealed." It consists of two parts.

First, the person who seals Christ with power and authority is God the Father. All the persons in the Godhead are equal in nature, power, and dignity, yet in their operation there is an order observed among them. The Father sends the Son, the Son is sent by the Father, and both send the Holy Spirit.

Second, the subject in whom the Father places His authority is Christ. The Father has so sealed Him as He never sealed anyone before Him or after Him: "There is none other name under heaven given among men, whereby we must be saved" (Acts 4:12); "The government shall be upon his shoulder" (Isa. 9:6).

Doctrine: Christ did not of Himself undertake the work of our redemption, but God the Father solemnly sealed Him unto it.

When I say that Christ did not undertake this work of Himself, I do not mean that He was unwilling to do it. His heart was as fully engaged as the Father's was (Ps. 40:7–8). What I mean is that He did not come without a full commission from His Father (John 8:42; Heb. 5:4–5). Our present business is to open Christ's commission and to view the great seal of heaven by which it was ratified. I will handle four points.

The Purpose of the Sealing
Christ was sealed to the whole work of mediation, to save all the elect whom the Father had given Him (Isa. 44:5; John 17:2; 1 Peter 3:18). More particularly, He was sealed to the offices of prophet, priest, and king in order to accomplish this glorious work. First, God sealed Him to His prophetic office, commissioning Him to preach the glad tidings of salvation to sinners (Luke 4:17–21). Second, God sealed Him to His priestly office, authorizing Him to execute both parts of it: oblation and intercession (John 19:18; Phil. 2:8; Heb. 7:21–25). Third, God called Him to His regal office. He was set upon the highest throne of authority by His Father's commission (Matt. 28:18).

The Implications of the Sealing
What does the Father's sealing of Christ imply? First, it implies the validity and efficacy of all His mediatory acts. This sealing fully ratified all that He did, and thus it is a source of

comfort and security. Everything that is done without commission and authority is null and void. But what is done by commission and authority is authentic. If Christ had come from heaven and entered upon His mediatory work without a due call, our faith would stumble at the very beginning.

Second, it implies the great obligation that was upon Christ to be faithful in His work. The Father placed a great trust upon Him and relied upon Him for its faithful discharge. Upon this account, Christ reckoned Himself to be obliged to pursue His Father's design (John 5:30; 9:4). His eye was always upon His Father's will, and He reckoned Himself to be under a necessity of precise and punctual obedience to it. As a faithful servant, He was willing to have His own will swallowed up in His Father's will.

Third, it implies Christ's complete qualification (or instrumental fitness) to serve the Father's design in our recovery. God will not seal an unfit person for His work. Whatever is desirable in a servant was eminently found in Christ: faithfulness (Heb. 3:2–6; Rev. 1:5), zeal (John 2:16–17; 4:32), love (Heb. 3:5–6), wisdom (Isa. 52:13), and self-denial (John 8:50). If He had not been all these things, He could never have been employed in this great work.

Fourth, it implies Christ's sole authority to appoint what He pleases in the church. This is His peculiar prerogative. God has sealed Christ, and none but Him (John 10:8). He foretells that some will labor to deceive the world with a pretend commission and counterfeit seal (Matt. 24:24). But God never commissioned anyone but Christ.

The Means of the Sealing

How did the Father seal Christ to this work? First, He sealed Him by solemn designation, meaning He singled Him out and set Him apart for it (Isa. 42:1; 1 Peter 2:4). This is implied in John 10:36, where we read that the Father sanctified Him—that is, separated Him and devoted Him to this service.

Second, the Father sealed Christ by unparalleled sanctification. He was anointed as well as appointed to it. The Lord filled Him with the Holy Spirit to qualify Him for this service (Isa. 61:1–3; Luke 4:1). He anointed Him "with the oil of gladness" above His fellows (Ps. 45:7). We are His fellows (or copartners) of the Holy Spirit. We too have an anointing, but not as Christ had it. It was poured out abundantly on Christ, our head, and it ran down to the hem of His garment (John 3:34). God filled Christ's human nature to the utmost capacity with all fullness of the Spirit of knowledge, wisdom, love, and so on for the effectual administration of His mediatorship. He was full *extensively* with all kinds of grace, and He was full *intensively* with all degrees of grace. "It pleased the Father that in him should all fulness dwell" (Col. 1:19), so that He might not only fill all things (Eph. 1:22) but that He might be fit in every way to discharge His work. The holy oil that was poured upon the heads of kings and priests, whereby they were consecrated to their offices, was typical of the Holy Spirit by whom Christ was consecrated (or sealed) to His offices.

Third, the Father sealed Christ by immediate testimony from heaven. He was declared to be the person whom the Father had solemnly designed and appointed to this work. God gave this extraordinary testimony at two remarkable seasons: (1) at the beginning of His ministry (Matt. 3:17) and

(2) at the beginning of His suffering (Matt. 17:5). With this voice, God owned, approved, and ratified Christ's work.

Fourth, the Father sealed Christ by extraordinary miraculous works. In these the Father gave convincing testimonies to the world that this was He whom He had appointed to be our Mediator (Matt. 11:3–5; John 5:36; Acts 10:38).

The Need for the Sealing

Why was it necessary for Christ to be sealed by His Father? First, it fulfills and accomplishes the types that prefigured Him. Under the law, the kings and priests had their inauguration by solemn anointing. This foreshadowed Christ's consecration (or sealing) (Heb. 5:4–5). Second, it engages us to love the Father because it reveals His love for us. If the Father had not sealed Christ with such a commission, Christ would not have come. But He did come in the Father's name and in the Father's love. We are bound, therefore, to ascribe equal glory and honor to them (John 5:23). Third, it causes us to ground our faith in Christ. How could we be satisfied that He is indeed the true Messiah unless He had shown His Father's seal upon Him? If He had come from heaven without these credentials, who would rest their faith in Him? "If I bear witness of myself, my witness is not true" (John 5:31). If He had only given His bare word as confirmation, and not produced any evidence from His Father, His testimony would have been invalid. But He has His Father's seal, and therefore all doubt is removed.

Application

Lesson 1

It is unreasonable to refuse to believe in Christ. He has revealed His commission in the gospel, shown the world His Father's seal upon it, and provided ample satisfaction. Yet even His own refused to receive Him (Isa. 53:1; John 1:11). When we consider the convincing evidence with which Christ comes, it is a mystery that anyone should not believe. We must adore the justice of God, permitting it to be so, giving people up to such unreasonable obstinacy. It is a sore plague that lies upon the world and a wonder that we are not engulfed in the same unbelief.

Lesson 2

It is a great sin to reject and despise those who are sent and sealed by Christ. As He came to us in His Father's name, so He has sent forth ministers by the same authority (John 17:18; 20:21). If we despise Christ's ministers, we are slighting the Father (who sent Christ) and Christ (who sent them). If we set ourselves against a minister of Christ, we set ourselves against God the Father and God the Son (Luke 10:16). God expects us to behave as if the word spoken to us was spoken by Him. He expects submission to His Word as it is proclaimed by His ministers. This reverence is not due to them as men, but as Christ's ambassadors. By the way, this instructs ministers that the best way to maintain their people's respect is to keep close to their commission.

Lesson 3

There is great efficacy in all gospel ordinances that are duly administered. Having received a full commission from His

Father, Christ instituted and appointed ordinances in the church. All the power in heaven is engaged to make them good, to confirm and ratify them (Matt. 18:18; 28:18–20). They are not human appointments. Our faith does not stand in the wisdom of men, but in the power of God. The Father has committed that power to Christ, and it is the fountain from which all gospel institutions flow. Christ has promised to be with His officers. Therefore, when we come to an ordinance, we do not come with slight thoughts but with great reverence and great expectation, remembering Christ is there to make all good.

Lesson 4

The love of the Father and the Son is wonderful. The Father sealed a commission for the death of His Son to save us. He could have set His seal to the sentence of our damnation rather than to a commission for His Son's humiliation. Was it not wonderful grace in Christ to accept such a commission, understanding fully its content? O the love of Christ for us! We should cry out with the enamored spouse: "Set me as a seal upon thine heart, as a seal upon thine arm: for love is strong as death; jealousy is cruel as the grave: the coals thereof are coals of fire, which hath a most vehement flame" (Song 8:6).

Lesson 5

The Father's sealing of Christ is a great comfort to us. God stands engaged, even by His own seal, to allow and confirm whatever Christ has done in the business of our salvation. On this ground, we may thus plead with God: "Lord, You have sealed Christ to this office, and therefore I depend upon it. You allow all that He has done and all that He has suffered for me, and You will make good all that He has promised me." We must get our interest in Christ sealed to us by the Holy Spirit or else we cannot enjoy the comfort of Christ's being sealed for us. The Holy Spirit seals in two ways. First, objectively, He seals us by working in us those graces that are the conditions of the promises. Second, subjectively, He seals us by shining upon His own work and helping us to discern it. We discern it by its effects: we are careful to avoid sin (Eph. 4:30), we love God (John 14:15), we are ready to suffer for Christ (Rom. 5:3–5), we are confident in approaching God (1 John 5:13–14), and we are humble before God (Gen. 17:1–3).

7

The Consecration of the Mediator

And for their sakes I sanctify myself.
—JOHN 17:19

Having assumed a body and received a commission, Christ then devoted Himself to His work. In the former sermon, we heard what the Father did for the advancement of our salvation. In this sermon, we will hear what the Son does. In our verse, we read that Christ sanctifies Himself. The word *sanctify* is not used here in the sense of cleansing (or purifying) that which is unclean. Rather, it signifies (1) Christ's separation (or setting apart) of Himself to be a sacrifice and (2) Christ's consecration (or dedication) of Himself to this holy use and service. He voluntarily offers Himself as a holy and unblemished sacrifice to the Father for our redemption.

The purpose of His sanctifying Himself was that we might be sanctified. Here we see that Christ's death wholly respects us. He did not offer Himself as other priests did, but so that we might be sanctified. Christ is so in love with holiness that, at the price of His blood, He will buy it for us.

Doctrine: Christ completely dedicated Himself to the work of a mediator for the sake of the elect.

This doctrine is like a glass in which the eye of faith may see Christ preparing Himself to be offered up to God for us.

The Implications of Christ's Consecration

First, it implies the personal union of the two natures in Christ. This was the sacrifice. "Through the eternal Spirit [he] offered himself without spot to God" (Heb. 9:14). By His incarnation, our nature has become "himself." No greater honor can be done to our nature, and no greater ground of comfort can be proposed to us.

Second, it implies the greatness and dreadfulness of the breach that sin had made between God and us. Nothing less than Christ's sacrifice of Himself could make atonement (Heb. 10:5). Even if our tears for sin were as numerous as the drops of rain that have fallen since the creation of the world, our repentance could not atone for sin.

Third, it implies Christ's voluntary undertaking of the work of redemption. He did not die out of compulsion, but out of choice. Thus, He is said to offer up Himself to God (John 10:18; Heb. 10:14). Though it is often said His Father sent Him and gave Him, Christ's heart was fully set on the work. He was under no constraint but that of His own love. He died out of choice, and He was a freewill offering.

Fourth, it implies Christ's pure and perfect holiness. He had no spot or blemish in Him (Heb. 7:26; 1 Peter 1:19). All other people bear a double spot: the spot of original sin and the spots of actual sins. But Christ had neither of these. He did not have the spot of original sin, because He came in a peculiar way into the world, and so escaped it. Nor did He have the spots of actual sins because His life was spotless and pure (Isa. 53:9). Though tempted externally to sin, He was never defiled in heart or practice. He came as near as He could for our sakes, yet still without sin (Heb. 4:15). To sanctify Himself as a sacrifice, He had to be as the law requires: pure and spotless.

Fifth, it implies the strength of Christ's love and the largeness of His heart toward poor sinners. He set Himself apart wholly and entirely for us, so that everything He did and suffered was in respect to us. He did not live a moment, perform an act, or speak a word except to promote the great design of our salvation. "For unto us a child is born, unto us a son is given" (Isa. 9:6). He would never have become the Son of man, except to make us the sons and daughters of God. God would not have come down in the likeness of sinful flesh except to raise up sinful man unto the likeness of God. All His miracles were for us, to confirm our faith (John 11:42). When He lived on earth, He lived for us. When He died, He died for us (Gal. 3:13). When He was hanged on the cursed tree, He was hanged for us. When He was buried, He was buried for us. When He rose again, He rose for us—"for our justification" (Rom. 4:25). When He ascended into glory, He ascended for us—to prepare a place for us (John 14:2). Now He is there for us—to "make intercession" for us (Heb. 7:25). When He returns again to judge the world, He will come for us—to be "glorified" in us (2 Thess. 1:10). He will come to gather us to Himself, that where He is, there we may be in soul and body forever. Thus, He did wholly bestow Himself (His time, life, death, etc.) upon us, living and dying for no other end but to accomplish this great work of salvation for us.

Sixth, it implies the substitutionary nature of Christ's death. When Aaron consecrated the sacrifice, it was set apart for the people (Lev. 16:21). Similarly, Christ stood in our room, to bear our burden (Isa. 53:6–7). As Aaron laid the iniquities of the people upon the goat, so our iniquities were laid on Christ—our pride, unbelief, hardness of heart, vain thoughts, and earthly mindedness. His death was in our place as well as for our good.

Seventh, it implies the extraordinariness of Christ's person. It reveals Him to be priest, altar, and sacrifice—all in one. His name might well be called "Wonderful." He sanctifies Himself according to both natures. He sanctifies Himself according to His human nature, which was the sacrifice upon the altar of His divine nature, for it is the altar that sanctifies the gift. As the three offices never met in one person before, so these three things never met in one priest before. The priests indeed consecrated the bodies of beasts for sacrifices, but they never offered up their own souls and bodies as a whole burnt offering as Christ did.

The Beneficiaries of Christ's Consecration

"Christ our Passover is sacrificed for us" (1 Cor. 5:7). "Christ also hath loved us, and hath given himself for us" (Eph. 5:2). This will be explained by way of three considerations.

First, Christ was not offered to God for His own sins. The priests had to offer sacrifices for themselves as well as for the people. But Christ did not need to offer a sacrifice for Himself (Heb. 7:27). He was most holy (Isa. 53:9). Since He was most holy, His death must either be an act of injustice or an act of justice in relation to others. He could never have suffered and died by the Father's hand if He had not been a sinner by imputation. All our sins were laid on Him, not intrinsically but by imputation (2 Cor. 5:21). It is evident, therefore, that Christ's sacrifice is a respective (or relative) thing.

Second, the Scriptures frequently call Christ's death a price (1 Cor. 6:20) and a ransom (Matt. 20:28). It relates, therefore, to those who are in bondage and captivity. But Christ was never in captivity; He was always in His Father's bosom. We were in cruel bondage under the tyranny of sin and Satan, and we alone have the benefit of this ransom.

Third, Christ's death must relate to believers or else He must have died in vain. Either His blood must be shed with respect to believers or (which is most absurd) shed as water upon the ground. It was for our sakes (as the verse says) that He sanctified Himself. And now we may say, "Lord, the condemnation was Yours, that the justification might be mine; the agony Yours, that the victory might be mine; the pain Yours, and the ease mine; the stripes Yours, and the healing balm mine; the vinegar and gall were Yours, that the honey and sweet might be mine; the curse was Yours, that the blessing might be mine; the crown of thorns was Yours, that the crown of glory might be mine; the death was Yours, that the life purchased by it might be mine. You paid the price that I might enjoy the inheritance."

Application
Lesson 1

It is reasonable for believers to set themselves apart for Christ. What He was, He was for us. What He did, He did for us. All that He suffered, He suffered for us. "I beseech you therefore, brethren, by the mercies of God, that ye present your bodies a living sacrifice, holy, acceptable unto God, which is your reasonable service" (Rom. 12:1). As our good was Christ's end, so His glory must be our end (Rom. 14:8; Phil. 1:21). This is what it means to be a Christian. A Christian is someone who is wholly dedicated to the Lord. What greater evidence can there be that Christ set Himself apart for us than our setting ourselves apart for Him?

This is the marriage covenant: "Thou shalt abide for me… and thou shalt not be for another man: so will I also be for thee" (Hos. 3:3). What a life is the life of a Christian! Christ is all for us, and we are all for Him. Blessed exchange! All Christ has is ours. His person is wonderful, but what He is, He is for us. His life was spent in labor and travail, but it was lived for us. Our person is vile, and not worthy of Christ's acceptance, but it is His. My soul (with every faculty), my body (with every member), my time, my gifts, and my talents are His.

Christ set Himself apart for us. Will we set ourselves apart for Him alone? We will never do so, until we can say, "Whom have I in heaven but thee? and there is none upon earth that I desire beside thee" (Ps. 73:25). He left the best and highest enjoyments (even those in His Father's bosom) to set Himself apart to die and suffer for us. Are we ready to leave the best and sweetest enjoyments in this world to serve Him (Matt. 10:37)? He was so wholly given up to our service that He did not refuse the worst and hardest part of it—even bleeding, groaning, and dying. His love for us sweetened all this to Him. Do we account "the reproach of Christ greater riches than the treasures in Egypt" (Heb. 11:26)?

Lesson 2

It is a horrid evil to use Christ or His blood as a common and unsanctified thing. The apostate is said to tread upon the Son of God, as if He were no better than the dirt under his feet, and to count His blood an unholy (or common) thing (Heb. 10:29). But woe to them who do so! They shall be counted worthy of something worse than dying without mercy.

As this is the sin of the apostate, so it is the sin of all those who approach the Lord's Supper without faith, thereby profaning it (1 Cor. 11:29). When we draw near to God in that ordinance, we must take heed to sanctify His name by discerning this most holy and deeply sanctified body of the Lord. It is sanctified beyond all creatures (angels and people), not only in respect of the Holy Spirit who filled Him without measure with inherent holiness but also in respect of its dedication to such a service as this.

Lesson 3

It is a choice pattern of love to the saints. We are called to imitate Christ by giving up ourselves to the service of others. We see here how His heart was affected to us, that He would sanctify Himself as a sacrifice for us. We too ought to lay down our lives for others (1 John 3:16).

Lesson 4

Our sanctification is a good evidence that Christ set apart Himself to die for us. He sanctified Himself in vain, unless we are sanctified. Only holy souls can claim the benefit of that great sacrifice. We must examine ourselves, therefore, to see if God's holiness is found in us (1 Peter 1:15).

First, God's holiness is universal. He is "holy in all his works" (Ps. 145:17). Whatever He does, it is done as becomes a holy God. He is holy not only in all things but at all times. We must, therefore, be holy in all things and at all times, too, if ever we expect the benefit of Christ's consecration. We must not be sometimes hot and sometimes cold, sometimes careful and sometimes careless, one day in a spiritual rapture and the next day in a fleshly frolic. "Be ye holy in all manner of conversation" (1 Peter 1:15).

Second, God's holiness is exemplary. Christ is the great pattern of holiness. We should be examples of holiness too. "Let your light so shine before men, that they may see your good works" (Matt. 5:16). As wicked men infect one another by their examples and diffuse their poison wherever they go, so we should disseminate godliness in all places and companies. Those who frequently converse with us, especially those of our own families, ought to receive a deeper taste of heavenliness every time they come near us.

Third, God delights in nothing but holiness and holy ones. He has set all His pleasure in the saints. Therefore, we should be holy as He is holy. There is this difference between God's choice and ours: He does not choose people because they are holy, but that they may become holy; but we choose those whom God has chosen and made holy to be our delightful companions (Ps. 16:3).

Fourth, God abhors all unholiness. We should do the same, so that we are like our Father in heaven. When the Spirit of holiness runs down upon us, it is a sweet evidence that Christ was sanctified for us. Holy ones may confidently lay the hand of their faith on the head of this great sacrifice and say, "Christ our Passover is sacrificed for us."

The Nature of Christ's Mediation

*And one mediator between God
and men, the man Christ Jesus*
—1 TIMOTHY 2:5

This verse informs us of the nature of Christ's astonishingly glorious work. It is the work of mediation between "God and men," managed by the sole hand of "the man Christ Jesus." Here we have a description of Christ the Mediator.

First, He is described by the work (or office) in which He is employed: "mediator." This term signifies a middle person (a fit and equal person) who comes between two people, who are at variance, to make peace. Such a middle person is Christ, who is able to arbitrate justly and give God His due without ruin to us.

Second, He is described by the singularity of His mediation: "one Mediator." Though there are many mediators of reconciliation among people, and many intercessors in a petitionary way between God and men, there is only one Mediator of reconciliation between God and men. To make more mediators than one is as impious as to make more Gods than one. There is one God and one Mediator between God and men.

Third, He is described by the nature and quality of His person: "the man Christ Jesus." He is described by His human nature, not only because it was in this nature that He paid our ransom but because it is a source of comfort and encouragement to us. Christ clothed Himself in our flesh, and He tenderly regards all our wants and miseries. Thus, we may safely trust Him with all our concerns. He will carefully mind them as His own, and He will be for us a merciful and faithful high priest in things pertaining to God.

Fourth, He is described by His names: "Christ Jesus." The name *Jesus* notes the work for which He came, while the name *Christ* notes the offices to which He was anointed. In the execution of these offices, He is our Jesus. The whole gospel is contained in the name *Jesus*. It is the light, nourishment, and medicine of the soul.

Doctrine: Christ is the true and only mediator between God and men.

We have come "to Jesus the Mediator of the new covenant" (Heb. 12:24). He is "the Mediator of the new testament" (Heb. 9:15). I could show you a host of Scriptures that affirm this very thing, but I will focus on four chief points.

The Meaning of Christ's Mediatorship
The word *mediator* refers to a middle person—one who interposes between two parties, who are at variance, to make peace. Christ is such a mediator in respect of His person and office. In respect of His person, He is a mediator because He has the same nature as God and us—true God and true man. Some call

this His *substantial* mediation. In respect of His office, He is a mediator because He transacts the business of reconciliation between God and us. Some call this His *operative* mediation. These do not constitute two kinds of mediation. Because of His *substantial* mediation, He is fit to stand between God and us, to make peace (His *operative* mediation).

At times, the word *mediator* signifies umpire, arbitrator, messenger, interpreter, reconciler, or peacemaker. Christ is the Mediator (the middle person) in all these senses in His work of reconciliation and intercession. He manages this mediation as follows. First, as an umpire (or arbitrator), Christ lays His hands upon both parties. He lays His hands upon God (so to speak) and says, "Father, will You be at peace with them and receive them into Your favor? If so, You will be fully satisfied for what they have done against You." And then He lays His hand upon us and says, "Poor sinner, do not be discouraged. You will be justified and saved." Second, as a messenger (or ambassador), Christ comes to impart the mind of God to us, and so He presents our desires to God. Third, as a surety (or pledge), Christ engages to satisfy God by giving Himself on our behalf. Christ is our Mediator by way of satisfaction, coming under our obligation to answer the law. He did this on the cross.

The Implication of Christ's Mediatorship

Christ is a mediator between God and us. This has a number of implications. First, it implies that there is a most dreadful breach between God and men. If this were not the case, there would have been no need for a mediator of reconciliation. There was indeed a sweet amity between God and men at one time, but it was quickly dissolved by sin. The wrath of God was kindled against man (Ps. 5:5), and they are filled with enmity against God (Rom. 1:30). This put an end to all friendly commerce between them.

Second, it implies that God's justice must be satisfied. The very purpose of Christ's mediation was to make peace by giving full satisfaction to the party that was wronged. Some people dream of a reconciliation with God that is founded, not upon satisfaction but upon the absolute mercy, goodness, and freewill of God. But God's Word never speaks of such a thing. It always speaks of a reconciliation that is worked to us through Christ (John 6:40; Acts 4:12; Eph. 1:4–8). We cannot imagine how God could exercise mercy to the prejudice of His justice if He were to reconcile us to Himself without full satisfaction. Indeed, mercy moved the heart of God toward us, but it found no way to vent itself for us but through the blood of Christ. God's justice was fully satisfied, and our misery was fully cured, in Christ alone. "God lost neither the severity of His justice in the goodness of His mercy, nor the goodness of His mercy in the exactness of His severity" (Augustine). For anyone to think that they can reconcile themselves to God by anything but faith in the blood of this mediator is vanity; moreover, it is destructive to the soul and offensive to the grace and wisdom of God. Peace of conscience can be settled on no other foundation than this: either the penalty must be levied on the delinquent or satisfaction must be made by his surety. Therefore, He who will be made a mediator of reconciliation between God and man must bring to God a price in His hand, and that price must be adequate to the offense and wrong done to Him.

Third, it implies that Christ's blood is of infinite value. It was sufficient in itself to stop the course of God's justice. It rendered Him abundantly satisfied and well pleased, even with those who were formerly His enemies (Col. 1:21–22). Surely, that which can cause the holy God, justly incensed against sinners, to lay aside all His wrath, take an enemy into His bosom, and establish such a peace as can never be broken is a most excellent and efficacious thing.

Fourth, it implies that Christ's heart was filled with ardent love for poor sinners. He does not only mediate by way of entreaty, begging for peace, but He mediates in the capacity of a surety by putting Himself under obligation to satisfy our debts. O how compassionately did His heart work toward us! When He saw the arm of justice lifted up to destroy us, He interposed Himself and received the stroke. Our Mediator, like Jonah, seeing the stormy sea of God's wrath, ready to swallow us up, cast Himself into the sea to appease the storm.

Fifth, it implies that Christ is fit to undertake this work. The Father called Christ to be the umpire and arbitrator, trusting His honor into His hands. Christ was invested with this office and power virtually, soon after the breach was made by Adam's fall (Gen. 3:15). From that moment until His incarnation, Christ was a virtual and effectual mediator. On that account, He is called "the Lamb slain from the foundation of the world" (Rev. 13:8). Ever since His incarnation, He has been an actual mediator.

The Validity of Christ's Mediatorship

How do we know that Christ is the true and only Mediator between God and men? First, He is revealed to us by God.

If God revealed Him, we must receive Him. "But to us there is but one God, the Father, of whom are all things, and we in him; and one Lord Jesus Christ, by whom are all things, and we by him" (1 Cor. 8:6). There is one God—that is, one supreme essence, the first spring and fountain of blessings. And there is one Lord Jesus Christ—that is, one mediator "by whom are all things, and we by him." All things, which come from the Father to us, come through Christ, and all our addresses ascend to the Father through Christ. "Neither is there salvation in any other: for there is none other name under heaven given among men, whereby we must be saved" (Acts 4:12). There is no other name—that is, no other person authorized in the whole world to be our Mediator.

Second, Christ alone is fit for, and capable of, this office. Only the One who has the divine nature and the human nature united in His single person is a fit mediator to lay His hand upon both God and men. God alone could support the sufferings that were exacted for satisfaction—a mere man would have melted like a moth before the fire.

Third, Christ alone is sufficient to reconcile the world to God by His blood. The virtue of His blood reached back as far as Adam and reaches forward to the end of the world. It will be as fresh, vigorous, and efficacious at the end of the world as it was at the first moment it was shed.

The Capacity of Christ's Mediatorship

The last thing to be explained is in what capacity Christ executes His mediatory work. We affirm that He performs it as God-man in both natures. Some people deny that Christ acted as mediator according to His divine nature. They deny that the divine nature exerted its virtue in His active and passive obedience. In so doing, they rob Christ's mediation of all its efficacy, dignity, and value. As mediator, did He not have the power to lay down His life and power to take it up again (John 10:17–18)? As mediator, did He not have all power in heaven and earth to institute ordinances and appoint officers in the church (Matt. 28:18)? As mediator, did He not have authority to baptize men with the Holy Spirit (Matt. 3:11)? As mediator, did He not have authority to keep those whom His Father gave Him (John 17:12)? Are these the effects of His mere human nature? Surely, He performs them as God-man. Furthermore, how can He be the object of our faith and adoration, if He is not God-man?

Application
Lesson 1
It is dangerous to reject Christ, the only Mediator between God and man. There is no one else to protect us from everlasting burnings. O it is a fearful thing to fall into the hands of the living God! Who can dwell with devouring fire? Who can endure the everlasting burnings? O we must take heed of despising or neglecting Christ! Apart from Christ, there is no one to intercede with God for us. The breach between Him and us can never be healed without Christ. If a person sins against God by despising Christ, who will entreat for him? What hope and remedy remain? Luther said, "I will have nothing to do with an absolute God"—that is, he will have nothing to do with God without a mediator.

Lesson 2

It is a great evil to join any other mediators, by way of reconciliation or intercession, with Christ. It pours the greatest contempt upon Christ, and it brings the surest destruction upon the sinner. Many stamp their own sordid works with the peculiar value and dignity of Christ's blood and therein seek to enter by the gate that God has shut to all the world. Because Christ has entered heaven in a direct and immediate way, in His own name and for His own sake, the gate is shut to all others. I wish people would consider it and fear, lest while they seek entrance into heaven at the wrong door, they do not forever shut against themselves the true and only door of happiness.

Lesson 3

We should thankfully ascribe all our peace, favor, and comfort to our Christ. When we have enjoyed free admission and sweet communion with God in the public ordinances or private duties of His worship, and when we have enjoyed His smiles and seals with hearts warmed with comfort, we should say, "O I may thank my Lord Jesus Christ for all this. If He had not interposed as a mediator of reconciliation, I could never have enjoyed friendly communion with God."

When Adam sinned, the door of communion with God was immediately locked. There was no more drawing near to God. It was Christ, the Mediator, who opened the door again. In Him we have "boldness and access with confidence" (Eph. 3:12). We can now come to God by a new and living way, consecrated for us through Christ's flesh (Heb. 10:10). Christ's human nature had a double use: it hid the glory of the holy of holies, and it gave entrance into it. Christ's incarnation softened the edge of the divine glory and brightness so that we are able to bear it and converse with it. We thank Christ for our present and future heaven. These are mercies that daily emerge out of the ocean of His blood.

Lesson 4
The condition of believers is secure. As Christ's mediation by suffering has fully reconciled, so His mediation by intercession will maintain the state of peace between God and us. "Being justified by faith, we have peace with God through our Lord Jesus Christ" (Rom. 5:1). It is a firm peace, and the Mediator (who made it) is now in heaven to maintain it (Heb. 9:24).

Here it is proper to reflect upon the profound and incomprehensible wisdom of God, who has made an advantage to us, even out of our sin and misery. He has so improved, reduced, and disposed the fall of Adam as to make a singular advantage thereby to advance His offspring to a better state. Adam's holiness was perfect, and his happiness was great, but neither of them was permanent. But our holiness and happiness (by the Mediator) are. "O how happily did I fall in Adam, who rose again happier in Christ" (Augustine). The Lord turned a poison into an antidote. The dreadful fall made way for a more blessed and fixed state. Now we are so confirmed and established in Christ, by the favor of God, that there can be no more such fatal breaches between God and His reconciled ones. Blessed be God for Jesus Christ!

The Prophet's Work of Revelation

A prophet shall the Lord your God raise up unto you of your brethren, like unto me; him shall ye hear in all things whatsoever he shall say unto you.
—ACTS 3:22

We proceed to consider how Christ executes His mediation in the discharge of His offices of prophet, priest, and king. His prophetical office consists of two parts. The first is external, consisting of His true and full revelation of the will of God to man (John 17:6). The second is internal, consisting of His illumination of the mind and inclination of the heart to receive and embrace His revelation. The first part is contained in the verse before us: "A prophet shall the Lord your God raise up." These words are taken from Deuteronomy 18:15. Peter applies them to Christ, to convince the incredulous Jews that He is the true Messiah and the great prophet of the church. There are two parts in these words.

First, there is a *description*: "A prophet shall the Lord your God raise up unto you of your brothers, like unto me." Here, Christ is described by His title: "prophet." He is the Prince of the prophets, or the Great and Chief Shepherd (Heb. 8:10;

1 Peter 5:4). It belongs to a prophet to expound the law, declare the will of God, and foretell things to come. All these come together in a singular and eminent manner in Christ (Matt. 5:17; John 1:18, 1 Peter 1:11).

Christ is also described by His type: "a prophet...like unto me [Moses]." There was so great a prophet in Israel as Moses, in respect of his familiarity with God and the miracles he performed by God's power. But, in comparison to Christ, Moses was but a star to the sun. However, Christ was like him in these following particulars. (1) He was a prophet that went between God and the people, declared God's mind to them, and expressed their mind to God (Deut. 18:16–18). (2) He was a faithful prophet, and exact in all that God entrusted to Him (Heb. 3:5–6). (3) He confirmed His doctrine by miracles, and He performed these in the presence of opponents. (4) He brought God's Israel out of Egypt.

Christ is also described by His stock: "of your brethren" (Rom. 9:5; Heb. 7:14). He honored that nation by His nativity.

Second, there is an *exhortation*: "him shall ye hear in all things whatsoever he shall say unto you." To "hear" is to obey. Obedience is to be yielded to Christ alone. It is true that we are commanded to obey the voice of His ministers (Heb. 13:17), but it is Christ who is speaking through them; thus, we obey them in the Lord. Our obedience to Christ is to be universal: "him shall ye hear in all things." His commands are to be obeyed, not disputed. We must "prove what is that good, and acceptable, and perfect, will of God" (Rom. 12:2). When His will is known and understood, we have no liberty to choose otherwise. Obedience is required under penalty of being destroyed from among the people.

Doctrine: Christ is called and appointed by God to be the great prophet and teacher of the church.

Christ is anointed to preach good tidings to the meek, and He is sent to bind up the brokenhearted (Isa. 61:1). When He came to preach the gospel among the people, He fulfilled Isaiah's prophecy: "All things are delivered unto me of my Father: and no man knoweth the Son, but the Father; neither knoweth any man the Father, save the Son, and he to whomsoever the Son will reveal him" (Matt. 11:27). All light is now collected into one body of light, the Sun of righteousness. He "lighteth every man that cometh into the world" (John 1:9). He dispensed knowledge variously in times past, speaking in many ways to the fathers, but now the way of revealing the will of God to us is fixed and settled in Christ. In these last times, God has spoken to us by His Son (Heb. 1:2). In this point, two things must be opened and discussed.

The Implication of Christ's Prophetical Office

What is implied in Christ's role as a prophet? First, it implies that people are naturally ignorant and blind in the things of God. They sit in the shadow of death until Christ shines upon their souls (Matt. 4:15–17). In the state of innocence, man had a clear apprehension of God's will. But now that light is quenched in the corruption of human nature (1 Cor. 2:14). The things of God are not only contrary to corrupt and carnal reason but they are above right reason. Grace indeed uses nature, but nature can do nothing without grace. The mind of a natural man has a native blindness, by reason of which it cannot discern the things of the Holy Spirit. It also has a natural enmity (Rom. 8:7). Until the mind is healed and enlightened by Christ, the natural faculty cannot discern the things of the Holy Spirit. The mysteries of nature may be discovered by the light of nature, but, when it comes to supernatural mysteries, the most searching and penetrating mind is at a loss.

Second, it implies that Christ is true God. Who else can reveal the secret counsels of God but He who eternally lay in the bosom of the Father (John 1:18; 8:38; 17:8)? Christ is a fixed and perpetual sun, who gives light in all ages of the world, for He is "the same yesterday, and to day, and for ever" (Heb. 13:8). Yea, the very beams of His divinity shone upon the hearts of those who heard Him, so that even His enemies were forced to acknowledge that "never man spake like this man" (John 7:46). Nature stands in need of grace for the right disposing of the mind to receive a supernatural object, and grace uses nature so that by strength of mind, clearness of judgment, and the light of good education, greater progress may be made in the study of the sacred writings.

Third, it implies that Christ is the original and fountain of all that light which is diffused by ministers. They are the stars that shine with a borrowed light from the sun. Those who teach others must first be taught by Christ. All the prophets of the Old Testament, and all the prophets, pastors, and teachers of the New Testament, have lit their candles at Christ's torch. It was Christ who gave them "a mouth and wisdom" (Luke 21:15). What Paul received from the Lord, he delivered to the church (1 Cor. 11:23). Christ is the Chief Shepherd (1 Peter 5:4), and all the undershepherds receive their gifts and commissions from Him.

The Execution of Christ's Prophetical Office

We shall next inquire as to how Christ executes and discharges His office—how He enlightens and teaches people. First, our Prophet has revealed God's will *variously* (Heb. 1:1). Sometimes He has taught the church immediately in His own person (John 18:20), and sometimes He has taught the church mediately by His ministers and officers. Before His incarnation, He dispensed the knowledge of God mediately to the church. It was Christ who, by the ministry of Noah, went and preached to the spirits in prison (1 Peter 3:19); that is, to men and women then alive but now separated from the body and imprisoned in hell for their disobedience. And it was Christ who was with the church in the wilderness, instructing and guiding them by the ministry of Moses and Aaron (Acts 7:38). And this is how He has taught the church since His ascension. He cannot be personally with us because He is in heaven, but He has appointed His officers in the church (Eph. 4:11–12).

Second, our Prophet has revealed God's will *gradually*. Sometimes the discoveries of light have been obscure: visions, dreams, oracles, types, sacrifices, and so on. They were but a glimmering light and had no glory compared to that which now shines (2 Cor. 3:7–11). It was sufficient for the instruction and salvation of the elect in those times, but now the light has shone gloriously in the gospel dispensation. It is not a twilight, but the light of a perfect day.

Third, our Prophet has revealed God's will *plainly*. While He was on earth, Christ taught the people by parables (Matt. 13:3–4). He clothed sublime and spiritual mysteries in earthly metaphors, bringing them to people's dull capacities. And so He would have His ministers preach, using "great plainness of speech" (2 Cor. 3:12). He would have us stoop to the understandings of the simplest and not give the people a comment darker than the text. He would have us pierce their ears rather than tickle their fancies and break their hearts rather than please their ears. Christ was a very plain preacher.

Fourth, our Prophet has revealed God's will *powerfully*. He spoke "as one having authority, and not as the scribes" (Matt. 7:29). They were cold and dull preachers, and their words froze between their lips. But Christ spoke with power. There was heat as well as light in His doctrine. The Word is "quick, and powerful, and sharper than any twoedged sword, piercing even to the dividing asunder of soul and spirit, and of the joints and marrow" (Heb. 4:12). The blessed apostle imitated Christ and, being filled with His Spirit, spoke freely to people's hearts. Faithful ministers are not similarly gifted in this particular, but there is a holy seriousness and spiritual grace and majesty in their doctrine, commanding reverence from their hearers.

Fifth, our Prophet revealed God's will *sweetly*. Christ spoke in an affectionate manner. His words made people's hearts burn within them (Luke 24:32). He did not break "a bruised reed" or quench "smoking flax" (Isa. 42:3). He spoke the word in season to the weary soul (Isa. 41:1). He gathered the lambs with His arm and gently led those that were with young (Isa. 40:11). How sweetly did His words slide into melting hearts! He drew with cords of love. He discouraged none who were willing to come to Him. Such is His gentle and sweet carriage to His people that the church is called the Lamb's wife (Rev. 19:7).

Sixth, our Prophet revealed God's will *purely*. Christ's doctrine did not have the least dash of error to debase it. His most envious hearers could find nothing to charge against Him. He is "the faithful witness" (Rev. 1:5). He has commanded His ministers to preserve the purity and simplicity of the gospel (2 Cor. 4:2).

Seventh, our Prophet revealed God's will *fully*. Christ kept nothing back that was necessary for salvation (John 15:15). He was faithful "as a son over his own house" (Heb. 3:6).

Application

Lesson 1

Believers require a standing ministry in the church. Christ now teaches us by His ministers, and He has fixed them in the church by a firm commission to remain to the end of the world (Matt. 28:20). His ministers supply the want of His personal presence. He gave them to the church at His ascension—that is, when He ceased to teach them with His own lips.

Lesson 2

The weakest believers do not need to be discouraged by the dullness they find in themselves. Christ is not only a patient teacher, but He can reveal to babes what is hidden from the wise and learned (Matt. 11:25). "The testimony of the LORD is sure, making wise the simple" (Ps. 19:7). Yea, the Lord delights to choose the simple, that His grace may be more conspicuous in our weakness (1 Cor. 1:26–27). Others may know more in other things than we do, but we are not incapable of knowing what is necessary to save our souls. If we know Christ and the truth as it is in Him, one drop of our knowledge is worth a whole sea of other people's natural abilities.

Lesson 3

Prayer is a proper means of increasing knowledge. Prayer is the golden key that unlocks that treasure. Martin Luther often insisted that three things made a divine: "meditation, temptation, and prayer." Those truths that are obtained by prayer leave an unusual sweetness upon the heart. If Christ is our teacher, it becomes all His saints to be at His feet.

Lesson 4

Believers know how to judge and discern doctrines. As Christ is holy, humble, heavenly, meek, peaceful, plain, simple, and in all things contrary to the wisdom of the world and the gratification of the flesh, so are the truths that He teaches. They have His character engraved on them. Would we know whether this or that doctrine is from the Spirit of Christ? We must examine it by this rule: whatever doctrine encourages sin; exalts self; accommodates earthly designs and interests; bends to the lusts of men; makes those who profess it carnal, turbulent, proud, or sensual did not come from Christ. His doctrine leads to godliness. His truth sanctifies.

Lesson 5

Believers may judge who are sent by Christ, the great prophet, to declare His will. Surely, those whom He sends have His Spirit in their hearts, as well as His words in their mouths. According to the measures of grace received, they faithfully endeavor to fulfill their ministry for Christ, as Christ did for His Father (John 20:21). They take Christ for their pattern in the whole course of their ministration and sincerely endeavor to imitate the Great Shepherd as follows. (1) Christ was a faithful minister (Rev. 1:5). He declared the whole mind of God (Ps. 40:10). The apostle Paul did the same (Acts 20:20, 35). Truth must be spoken, even if the greatest on earth are offended (Gal. 1:10; 1 Thess. 2:4). (2) Christ was a tenderhearted minister. He was full of compassion (Isa. 61:1; Matt. 23:37; Mark 3:5). The same compassion must be in all His undershepherds (Phil. 1:8). He who has a hard heart and remains unaffected with the dangers and miseries of others can never show a commission from Christ to authorize him for ministerial work. (3) Christ was a laborious minister (John 9:4; Acts 10:38). He was never idle. His ministers must resemble Him in this (Col. 1:28–29). An idle minister is a contradiction in terms, as if we should speak of a dark light. (4) Christ delighted in nothing more than the success of His ministry (Luke 10:17–18). It is the same for those who are sent by Him. They value the success of their ministry at a high rate. (5) Christ was a minister who lived up to His doctrine (Matt. 11:28). Likewise, His ministers desire to approve themselves (Phil. 4:9). He preached to their eyes as well as their ears. His life was a comment on His doctrine. (6) Christ was a minister who minded and maintained sweet and secret communion with God (Matt. 14:23). Let the keepers of the vineyards remember they have a vineyard of their own to keep, a soul to look after. Those who imitate Christ in these things are surely sent to us from Him and are worthy of double honor. They are a choice blessing to the people.

10

The Prophet's Work of Illumination

Then opened he their understanding, that they might understand the scriptures.
—LUKE 24:45

Knowledge of spiritual things is well distinguished into *intellectual* and *practical*. The first has its seat in the mind, but the second has its seat in the heart. Divines maintain that this second kind of knowledge is peculiar to the saints. It is "the knowledge of Christ" (Phil. 3:8). Light in the mind is necessarily antecedent to the heavenly motions and elevations of the affections. The farther people stand from the light of truth, the farther they are from the heat of comfort. Heavenly quickening is begotten in the heart, while the Sun of righteousness spreads the beams of truth into the understanding. Yet all the light of the gospel, spreading and diffusing itself into the mind, can never change the heart without another act of Christ upon it: "Then opened he their understanding, that they might understand the scriptures." There are two points in this verse.

First, there is the *nature* of Christ's act: "Then opened he their understanding." In this case, the "understanding" does not refer to the mind in opposition to the heart, will, and affections. It refers to all these. The mind is to the heart as the door is to the house. What comes into the heart comes through the mind. The two doors of the soul are barred against Christ: the mind by ignorance and the heart by hardness. But Christ opens both. The first is opened by the preaching of the gospel, and the second is opened by the internal operation of the Holy Spirit. The first belongs to the first part of Christ's prophetical office, and the second belongs to the second part of His prophetical office. The fact that Christ opened their hearts as well as their minds is evident in the effects: they returned to Jerusalem "with great joy" and they were "praising and blessing God" in the temple (Luke 24:52–53).

Second, there is the *end* of Christ's act: "that they might understand the scriptures." God never intended to abolish His Word by giving His Spirit. And they are true fanatics who claim otherwise.

Doctrine: The opening of the mind and heart to receive God's truth is Christ's peculiar office and prerogative.

Spiritual blindness is one of the great miseries under which fallen nature labors. Christ brings the only remedy that can cure it (Rev. 3:18). It is not enough that the object is revealed or that the subject has a due use of his own reason. The special assistance of the Holy Spirit is absolutely necessary to open and soften the heart, and so give it a due taste and relish of the sweetness of spiritual truth. He must open the mind, revealing truth to us, and open the heart, revealing truth in us. This is the special blessing promised in the new covenant (Heb. 8:10).

The Implication of Christ's Prophetical Office

What is implied in Christ's act of illumination? First, it implies that spiritual things far exceed the reach of natural reason. Christ must by His Spirit open our understandings, or else we can never comprehend such mysteries (1 Cor. 1:20). Surely, it is possible for a person to dispute every point of knowledge and yet be as blind as a bat in the knowledge of Christ. Yea, it is possible for a person's understanding to be improved by the gospel to a great ability in the literal knowledge of it so as to be able to expound the Scriptures and enlighten others by them (Matt. 7:22). But until Christ opens the heart, we can know nothing of Him or His will (1 Cor. 2:14–15). A person who carries a dark lantern can see another person by its light, but the other person cannot discern him. Such is the difference between those whose hearts Christ has or has not opened.

Second, it implies that all external means are insufficient. No matter how excellent they are in themselves, they cannot operate effectively upon us until Christ opens the soul, thereby making them effectual. Isaiah was a great preacher, yet he complains, "Who hath believed our report? and to whom is the arm of the LORD revealed?" (Isa. 53:1). Who enjoyed such choice means as those who lived under the ministry of Christ and the apostles? Yet how many of them remained in darkness (Matt. 11:27)? Neither the delightful offers of mercy nor the doleful threats of judgment could move their hearts. The best means can do nothing upon the heart until Christ by His Spirit opens it. The efficacy of the means depends upon the gracious concurrence of the Holy Spirit (John 3:8). When He comes down at certain times in the Word, and opens the heart, then it becomes the power of God to salvation.

Third, it implies that people are incapable of opening their hearts, thereby making the Word effectual to their conversion and salvation. He who said, "Let there be light" must shine into our hearts, or they will never be enlightened (2 Cor. 4:4–6). A double misery lies upon humanity: impotency and pride. People have not only lost the liberty of their wills but they have lost the humility to admit it. They have become impotent creatures as a result of the fall. They cannot know the things of the Holy Spirit (1 Cor. 2:14). They cannot believe (John 6:44). They cannot obey (Rom. 8:7). They cannot speak one good word (Matt. 12:34). They cannot think one good thought (2 Cor. 3:5). They cannot perform one good act (John 15:5). This is why conversion is called a regeneration (John 3:3), resurrection (Eph. 2:5), and creation (Eph. 2:10). This implies not only that people are passive in their conversion to God but that they are completely opposed to that power which goes forth from God to recover them.

Fourth, it implies that Christ is able to subdue all things to Himself. We may stand and knock at people's hearts, but they will not open until Christ comes. With sweet efficacy, He can open any soul and do so without any force or violence to it.

The Execution of Christ's Prophetical Office

How does Christ perform His work in opening the hearts of sinners? There are two principal means. The first is His Word. The apostle Paul was commissioned to preach the gospel: "to open their eyes, and to turn them from darkness to light, and from the power of Satan unto God" (Acts 26:18). If He pleases, Christ can accomplish this immediately. But He ordinarily chooses to work by means. Thus, we read that, when

Lydia's heart was to be opened, "a vision appeared to Paul in the night." A man from Macedonia pleaded with him: "Come over into Macedonia, and help us" (Acts 16:9). God will use His ordinances among us. Though He has not tied Himself to them, He has tied us to them.

The second means by which Christ opens the hearts of sinners is His Spirit. The ordinances in themselves cannot do it; therefore, Christ has sent forth the Holy Spirit to carry on this work in the hearts of His elect. When the Holy Spirit comes down upon His people in the administration of the ordinances, He effectually opens their hearts to receive Christ by the hearing of faith. He breaks in upon the understanding and conscience by powerful convictions (John 16:8). Yet the door of the heart is not opened until He has also put forth His power upon the will, and by a sweet and secret efficacy overcome all its objections. Thus, the soul is made willing in the day of His power. When this is done, the heart is opened, and saving light now shines upon it.

It is a *new* light, in which all things appear far different than they did before. The names *Christ* and *sin* and the words *heaven* and *hell* have a different sound in our ears than they had before. When we come to read the Scriptures, which we had possibly read a hundred times before, we wonder how we could have been so blind as to overlook such great and weighty tidings.

It is also an *affecting* light. It has powerful influences with it, which make deep impressions on the heart. The soul is greatly affected with what it sees. The beams of light are contracted and twisted together in the mind and, being reflected on the heart and affections, soon cause them to smoke and burn.

Finally, it is a *growing* light. It is like the light of the morning that "shineth more and more unto the perfect day" (Prov. 4:18). When the Holy Spirit first opens the understanding, He does not give it at once a full sight of all truths or a full sense of the power, sweetness, and goodness of any truth. Rather, by the use of means, the soul grows up to a greater clearness day by day. Its knowledge grows extensively in measure and intensively in power and efficacy.

Application
Lesson 1
Spiritual blindness is a miserable condition (2 Cor. 4:4). Because this point is of such deep concernment, let us carefully consider the following points. First, the *nature* of this judgment: spiritual blindness. This is a sore misery indeed. It is not a universal ignorance of all moral and natural truth, but of the truth that relates to eternal life (John 17:2–3). The natural man is very learned in other matters, but he does not know Christ. Second, the *subject* of this judgment: the mind. Spiritual blindness falls immediately upon the soul, the noblest part of man, and upon the mind, the highest and noblest faculty of the soul, whereby we think, reason, and understand. In Scripture, it is called the "spirit"—the intellectual or rational faculty, which the philosophers call the leading directive faculty. The mind is to the soul what the eye is to the body. Given its directive power, it is a sad and dangerous state to be spiritually blind. Third, the *subtlety* of this judgment: indiscernible. People do not know it any more

than they know they are asleep. Indeed, it is "the spirit of deep sleep" poured out upon them by the Lord (Isa. 29:10). It renders their misery the more remediless: "But now ye say, We see; therefore your sin remaineth" (John 9:41). Fourth, the *effect* of this judgment: eternal ruin. The soul that is blinded can never see sin or a savior. It considers all the duties and ordinances, by which illumination comes, to be useless. They come to the Word, and see others melted by it, but it means nothing to them. O this is a most wretched case!

Lesson 2
Those who are in darkness must apply themselves to Christ for saving knowledge. It is Christ alone who can cure spiritual blindness. He alone has the key of the house of David. He opens, and no one shuts. We must set ourselves in His way, under the ordinances, and cry to Him: "Lord, that my eyes may be opened!" There are three things that encourage us to do so.

First, it is encouraging to think that the Father has put Christ into this office to cure such as us (Isa. 49:6). This furnishes us with an argument to plead for a cure. Why do we not go to God and say, "Lord, did You give Christ a commission to open blind eyes? Look at me, Lord, I am a poor, dark, ignorant soul. Did You give Him to be Your salvation to the ends of the earth? And will I still remain in the shadow of death? O that He might be a saving light unto me!"

Second, it is encouraging to think that Christ has actually opened the eyes of those who were as dark and ignorant as we are. He has revealed those things to babes that have been hidden from the wise and learned (Matt. 11:25). The law of the Lord is perfect, "making wise the simple" (Ps. 19:7). If we look among those whom Christ has enlightened, we will find "not many wise men after the flesh, not many mighty, not many noble," but the "foolish," "weak," "base," and "despised" (1 Cor. 1:26–28).

Third, it is encouraging to think that God has mercifully preserved us under the means of light. Why are times and seasons of grace continued to us if God has no design of good to us? We must not be discouraged but wait on the Lord in the use of means, that we may yet be healed. The Holy Spirit can make those means effectual if He pleases to concur with them. It is true that our inability to do what is above our power to do in no way excuses us from doing what is within our power to do. Therefore, I advise us to (1) attend diligently upon an able, faithful, and searching ministry; (2) consider carefully what we hear; and (3) confess honestly the insufficiency of all our other knowledge to do us good. All our knowledge signifies nothing until the Lord shows us by special light the deplorable sight of our own heart and a saving sight of Christ— our only remedy.

Lesson 3
Since there is a common light and a special saving light, which only Christ can give, it is our duty to test what light we have. "We know that we all have knowledge" (1 Cor. 8:1), but where does it come from? Is it the light of life springing from Christ, the bright and morning star, or is it only that which the demons and damned have?

These lights differ in their *natures*. The one is heavenly, supernatural, and spiritual, while the other is earthly and natural (James 3:15–17).

These lights also differ in their *operations*. The light of Christ is humbling and abasing in that it reveals the vileness of our nature and practice; but natural light makes the heart swell with self-conceit (1 Cor. 8:1). The light of Christ is practical and operative, lovingly constraining us to obedience (Col. 1:6); but natural light is detained in unrighteousness (Rom. 1:18). The light of Christ is powerfully transformative, changing us into His image (2 Cor. 3:18); but natural light leaves the heart dead, carnal, and sensual, as if no light were in it at all. In a word, all saving light endears Christ to us. We could not value Him before we saw Him. But now that He appears to us in His own light, He is deeply appreciated. There is nothing in heaven or earth that is desirable in comparison to Him. But no such effect flows from natural knowledge.

Finally, these lights differ in their *issues*. Natural knowledge vanishes (1 Cor. 13:8). It is but a flower in May, which dies within a month. But the knowledge of Christ is perfected by death because it springs up into everlasting life. This light is life eternal (John 17:2).

Lesson 4

Those who have been enlightened with the saving knowledge of Christ are obliged to love, serve, and honor Him. How many around us have their eyes closed and their hearts locked? How many are in darkness? O what a pleasant thing it is for our eyes to see the light of the world! What is it for the eye of our mind to see God in Christ? We must be careful not to sin against the best and brightest light in this world. If God were incensed against the heathens for disobeying the light of nature, what is it for us to sin with eyes clearly illuminated with the purest light that shines in this world? When He opened our eyes, Christ intended for our eyes to direct our feet. Light is a special help to obedience, and obedience is a singular help to increase our light.

11

The Nature and Necessity of Christ's Priesthood

It was therefore necessary that the patterns of things in the heavens should be purified with these; but the heavenly things themselves with better sacrifices than these.
—HEBREWS 9:23

Salvation is revealed by Christ as a prophet, procured by Him as a priest, and applied by Him as a king. It is revealed in vain if it is not purchased, and it is revealed and purchased in vain if it is not applied. We have considered how it is revealed to us and in us by our great prophet. Now we proceed to Christ's priestly office. It contains great relief for those who are distressed by the guilt of sin. It is the blood of this great sacrifice, sprinkled by faith upon the trembling conscience, that must cool, refresh, and sweetly settle it.

Since a great weight hangs upon this office, the apostle diligently confirms and commends it in his epistle to the Hebrews. In the ninth chapter, he shows how it was prefigured by the blood of the Old Testament sacrifices while infinitely excelling them all. The blood of these sacrifices only purified the types (or patterns) of the heavenly things, but the blood of Christ's sacrifice purified (or consecrated) the heavenly things themselves.

There are two things to be especially observed in this verse. First, the nature of Christ's death: it was a most excellent sacrifice. Second, the need for Christ's death: it was necessary to expiate for sin, propitiate a justly incensed God, and open a way for reconciled ones to come to God.

Doctrine: The sacrifice of Christ, our High Priest, is most excellent in itself and most necessary for us.

My present design is to open the general nature and absolute necessity of Christ's priesthood, showing what it implies and how it was essential to secure our recovery from a deplorable state of sin and misery.

The Implications of Christ's Priesthood

First, Christ's priesthood implies that there is a dreadful breach between God and man. In all the sacrifices from Adam to Christ, this breach was preached to the world. The fire, flaming on the altar, which consumed the whole sacrifice, was a lively emblem of God's fiery indignation that should devour His adversaries. Above all these, our sin and misery by the fall was revealed when Christ, the true and great sacrifice, was offered up to God on the cross.

Second, Christ's priesthood implies that God's unalterable purpose is to take vengeance for sin. He will not let it pass. He must punish it in the person of the sinner or in the person of a surety. Those who contend for forgiveness as an act of charity must suppose that God surrenders His right to justice. They make Christ's satisfaction altogether useless, as to the procurement of forgiveness. Surely, God's nature obliges Him to punish sin. He is of "purer eyes than to behold evil" and He "canst not look on iniquity" (Hab. 1:13).

Third, Christ's priesthood implies that people are utterly incapable of appeasing God and recovering His favor by anything they can do. Surely, God would not have assumed a body to die for us if our redemption could have been accomplished at a cheaper rate. There was no other way to recover man and satisfy God. Those who deny Christ's satisfaction and speak of His dying merely to provide an example of meekness, patience, and self-denial do not only root up the foundations of their own peace, comfort, and pardon but boldly disparage God's infinite wisdom. Who can satisfy God? Who can bring Him an adequate and proportionate value for sin? Surely, Christ alone can do this.

Fourth, Christ's priesthood implies that He needed to be both God and man. It was necessary for Him to be a man for the derivation of His righteousness and holiness to people. If He had not been a man, He would not have had a sacrifice to offer, no soul or body in which to suffer. The Godhead is immortal and above all the sufferings and miseries Christ felt for us. In addition, as a man, He was filled with bowels of compassion and a tender sense of our miseries. This makes Him a merciful and faithful high priest (Heb. 4:15), and it fits Him to pity and sanctify us (Heb. 2:11, 14, 17). And it was necessary for our High Priest to be God, since the value and efficacy of His sacrifice results from His divinity.

Fifth, Christ's priesthood implies that His suffering was extreme. In the Old Testament sacrifices, there was a destruction (a kind of annihilation) of the creature to the glory of God. The shedding of the creature's blood, and the burning of its flesh with fire, was a faint resemblance of what Christ endured when He made His soul an offering for sin.

Sixth, Christ's priesthood implies that God's gracious design is to reconcile us at a dear rate to Himself. He called and confirmed Christ in His priesthood by an oath and thereby laid out a sacrifice of infinite value for the world. The case of sinners is helpless. But if God Himself provides a sacrifice, it plainly speaks of His intention to impart peace and mercy.

The Necessity of Christ's Priesthood
I affirm that Christ's priesthood was necessary in order to secure our salvation. The truth of this assertion is evident from these two principles: (1) God stood upon full satisfaction and would not remit one sin without it, and (2) fallen man is totally incapable of tendering Him any such satisfaction. Therefore, Christ (who alone can) must do it, or else we perish.

First, God stood upon full satisfaction and would not remit one sin without it. (1) The nature of sin deserves that the sinner should suffer for it. Penal evil, in a course of justice, follows moral evil (Rom. 6:23). (2) The veracity of God requires it. The word has gone out from His mouth: "In the day that thou eatest thereof thou shalt surely die" (Gen. 2:17). From that time, man was instantly and certainly liable to the death of soul and body. The law pronounces him cursed (Gal. 3:10). God will be true to His threats. (3) The wisdom of God requires it. By His wisdom, He governs the rational world, and He does not relax His threats without satisfaction. How could it be expected that people should fear and tremble before God, when they find themselves more scared than hurt by His threats against sin?

Some suggest that reconciliation upon full satisfaction is derogatory to the riches of God's grace and that we do not allow God to do what we do—namely, to forgive an injury freely without satisfaction. Free forgiveness to us and full satisfaction made to God by Christ for us are not inconsistent with each other. As for denying to God what we allow to people, we must remember that people stand on even ground. We are not as capable of being wronged by man as God is by man. There is no comparison between the nature of the offenses.

Second, we cannot render to God any satisfaction for the wrong we have done. There is no way to make amends to God, either by doing or suffering. (1) We cannot do it by doing. No one can satisfy God, or reconcile himself to Him, by what he does, for our best works are sinful (Isa. 64:6). If we do anything that is good, we are beholden to grace for it (John 15:5; 1 Cor. 15:10; 2 Cor. 3:5). The apostle Paul lived a holy, fruitful, and heavenly life, yet he says, "I know nothing by myself; yet am I not hereby justified" (1 Cor. 4:4). His sincerity might comfort him, but it could not justify him. The Lord has shut up this way to all the world: "Therefore by the deeds of the law there shall no flesh be justified in his sight" (Rom. 3:20). (2) We cannot do it by suffering. As we can never reconcile ourselves to God by doing, so we can never do it by suffering. The only suffering that can satisfy God is that which is proportionate to the offense. An infinite suffering must be borne, for sin is an infinite evil as it wrongs an infinite God. No one can bear the wrath of an infinite God.

Thus, we see that we cannot be our own priest, to reconcile ourselves to God by what we do or suffer. And, therefore, we require someone, who is able by doing and suffering to reconcile us to God, to undertake it for us.

Application
Lesson 1
The Reformed Christian religion is incomparably excellent. What other religions seek, only the Christian religion finds: a solid foundation for true peace of conscience. The Jew seeks it in the law, the Muslim in his external observance, and the papist in his own merit. But the believer finds it in the blood of this great sacrifice. This alone can pacify a distressed conscience, laboring under the weight of its own guilt. Conscience demands no less to satisfy it than God demands to satisfy Him. Those who pine away in their iniquities, drooping from day to day under the dismal wounds of conscience, can only find peace when they are persuaded to come to Christ's blood for sprinkling.

The blood of this sacrifice speaks better things than the blood of Abel. The blood of this sacrifice is the blood of God (Acts 20:28). It is incomparably precious (1 Peter 1:18–19). One drop excels the blood of all creatures (Heb. 10:4–6). What is the blood of beasts to God? The blood of all the people in the world can do nothing in this case. What is our polluted blood worth? It is the blood of God alone that must satisfy. Yea, Christ's blood is not only the blood of God, but it is the blood that is shed in our place (Gal. 3:13). It is, therefore, sin-pardoning blood (Rom. 3:26; Eph. 1:7; Col. 1:14; Heb. 9:22) and, consequently, conscience-pacifying and soul-quieting blood (Eph. 2:13–14; Col. 1:20). O bless God that ever the news of this blood came to our ears!

Lesson 2

Faith is necessary to arrive at a state and sense of peace with God. For what purpose is Christ's blood shed unless it is actually and personally applied and appropriated by faith? When the sacrifices under the law were brought to be slain, the individual put his hand upon the head of the sacrifice. And so it was accepted for him to make atonement (Lev. 1:4). It noted the putting off of his sins, and the penalty due to him for them, upon the head of the sacrifice. We must also lay the hand of faith upon Christ, our sacrifice, to apply and appropriate Him to ourselves.

The gospel persuades sinners to apply Christ and His blood to their souls (Matt. 11:28). By looking to the brazen serpent, the Israelites were healed (John 3:14–15). Likewise, we are healed by believing (or looking to Christ in faith). It is true that Christ's death is the meritorious cause of remission, but faith is the instrumental cause. As Christ's blood is necessary in its place, so also is our faith in its place. As there is God's love for the efficient cause, and Christ's death for the meritorious cause, so of necessity there must be faith for the instrumental cause. And these causes sweetly meet in their influences and activities in our remission and peace of conscience, and they are in their kind and place absolutely necessary to the procuring and applying of it. The death of Christ, and the offers of Christ, never saved one person without believing application.

I am assured that until God shows us the face of sin in the glass of the law, and until we have had some sick nights and sorrowful days for sin, we will never seek with tears an interest in the blood of Christ's sacrifice. But, if this is our condition, then we will know the worth of Christ and we will value the sprinkling of His blood.

Lesson 3
Christ's priesthood is indispensably necessary to our salvation. We must freely acknowledge our utter impotency to reconcile ourselves to God by anything we can do or suffer. Christ must have the whole glory of our recovery ascribed to Him. It is highly reasonable that He who laid down the whole price should have the whole praise. If anyone thinks he could have made an atonement for himself, he casts reproach upon that profound wisdom which laid the design of our redemption in Christ's death.

Lesson 4
We see the necessity of this Priest and His most excellent sacrifice, and accordingly we make use of it. The best of us have polluted natures, poisoned in the womb with sin. Our natures need this sacrifice. We must have the benefit of this blood to pardon and cleanse us. Our actual sins have need of the Priest and His sacrifice to procure remission for them. If He takes them not away by the blood of His cross, they can never be taken away. They will lie down with us in the dust. They will rise with us and follow us to the judgment seat, crying, "We are your works, and we will follow you." Our tears of repentance, were they as many as the drops in the ocean,

can never take away sin. Our duties, even the best of them, need this sacrifice. It is in its virtue that they are accepted by God. If God had no respect to Christ's offering, He would not regard us or any of our duties. We could no more come near to God than we could approach a devouring fire or dwell with everlasting flames.

Well then, we should confess that we need this sacrifice in every way, and we should love Christ in all His offices. God has been so good in providing such a sacrifice for us. Our hearts should be enlarged as we meditate on the excellency of Christ, which is thus displayed and unfolded in every branch of the gospel. Blessed be God for Jesus Christ!

12

The Priest's Oblation

For by one offering he hath perfected for ever them that are sanctified.
—HEBREWS 10:14

We have taken a general view of Christ's priesthood. We must now consider its parts: oblation and intercession. These correspond to the double office of the high priest. His offering of the blood of the sacrifices outside the holy place typified Christ's oblation, while His bringing the blood into the most holy place, presenting it before God and sprinkling it on the mercy seat, typified Christ's intercession.

My present business is to open and apply Christ's oblation. Its efficacy and excellency are commended to us in this verse: "For by one offering he hath perfected for ever them that are sanctified." It is "one offering," never to be repeated (Rom. 6:9). By it He has "perfected" us. It brings in a complete and perfect righteousness. All that remains to make us perfectly happy is the full application of the benefits procured by this oblation. The apostle commends it from its extensiveness; it is not restrained to a few but is applicable to all the saints in all ages and places. He also commends it from its perpetuity; it perfects forever. It will abide to the end of the world as fresh, vigorous, and powerful, as it was the first moment it was offered up.

Doctrine: Christ's oblation is of unspeakable value and everlasting efficacy to perfect all those who are (or will be) sanctified to the end of the world.

All of God's blessings flow from this oblation. Without it, there would be no justification, adoption, salvation, peace with God, hope of glory, pardon of sin, or divine acceptance. These things could never have had any real existence if Christ had not offered up Himself as a sacrifice to God for us (Heb. 9:14). His appearing before God as our priest, with such an offering for us, is what removes our guilt and fear (Heb. 9:28). We must apply our minds to a consideration of this excellent Priest who appears before God.

Christ's Person

The priest who appears before God with an oblation for us is Christ, God and man. The dignity of His person imparts inestimable worth to His offering. There were many priests before Him, but none like Him, either for the purity of His person or the perpetuity of His priesthood. They were sinful men, and they offered sacrifices for their own sins as well as the sins of the people (Heb. 5:3); but Christ was "holy, harmless, undefiled, separate from sinners" (Heb. 7:26). He could stand before God, even in the eye of His justice, as a lamb without spot. Though He made His soul an offering for sin, He "had done no violence, neither was any deceit in his mouth" (Isa.

53:9). Indeed, His offering would have done us no good, if the least taint of sin had been found on Him. They were mortal men (Heb. 7:23), but Christ is "a priest for ever" (Ps. 110:4).

Christ's Oblation

Christ's oblation (or offering) was not the blood of beasts, but His own blood (Heb. 9:12). He transcended all other priests because He had something of His own to offer. He offered His body (Heb. 10:10); yea, His soul was made "an offering for sin" (Isa. 53:10). It was necessary that Christ's sacrifice should be answerable to the debt we owed. And when Christ came to offer His sacrifice, He stood not only in the capacity of a priest but also in that of a surety. And so, His soul stood in the stead of our souls and His body in the stead of our bodies. Now, the excellency of this oblation will appear in the following properties.

First, it was *precious* (1 Peter 1:19). Being offered as an expiatory sacrifice, Christ's oblation was equivalent in its own intrinsic value to all the souls and bodies that were to be redeemed by it. There was a surplus of merit, which went to make a purchase for the redeemed. As one diamond is worth more than a thousand pebbles, and one piece of gold is worth more than many coins, so the soul and body of Christ are much more excellent than all the souls and bodies in the world.

Second, it was *complete*. Christ's oblation fully expiated the sins of all for whom it was offered, in all ages of the world. The virtue of this sacrifice reaches back as far as Adam and reaches forward to the last person of the elect. That its efficacy reached back to Adam is plain, for Christ is "the Lamb slain from the foundation of the world" (Rev. 13:8). As the sun at midday extends its light, not only forward toward the west but also backward toward the east, so did this most efficacious sacrifice reach all the elect who died before Christ's incarnation. It is, therefore, a vain quibble when some say that Christ's satisfaction was needless because many were saved without it. They argue that the effect cannot be before the cause. While this is true of physical causes, it is not the case with moral causes. Christ was engaged to the Father to satisfy for them, and upon that security they were delivered.

The virtue of this oblation not only reaches those believers who lived before Christ's day but it extends itself forward to the end of the world. Christ is said to be "the same yesterday, and to day, and for ever" (Heb. 13:8). He is a savior both to them and us. God has appointed the accomplishment of the promise to send the Messiah to be in the last times, so that those who lived before Christ should not be perfected (that is, justified and saved) by anything done in their time, but by looking to our time and Christ's satisfaction (Heb. 11:40). No passage of time can wear out the virtue of this eternal sacrifice. It is as fresh, potent, and vigorous now as the first hour it was offered. And though He actually offers it no more, He virtually continues it by His intercession in heaven.

The virtue of this oblation reaches backward and forward to all ages and all believers. It also reaches to all the sins of all believers, which it fully purges and expiates. No other oblation can do this. The legal sacrifices were not real expiations, but remembrances of sins (Heb. 9:9, 12; 10:3). Their virtue consisted in their typical relation to Christ's sacrifice (Heb. 9:13). His blood cleanses from all sin (1 John 1:7)—original and actual. It expiates all fully (without exception) and finally (without revocation). By His being made sin for us, we are made "the righteousness of God in him" (2 Cor. 5:21).

Third, it was *acceptable*. Christ's oblation was highly pleasing and delightful in God's eyes. He "hath given himself for us an offering and a sacrifice to God for a sweetsmelling savour" (Eph. 5:2). This does not mean that God took any delight in Christ's bitter suffering in itself considered, but in the end for which He was offered, even our redemption and salvation. This made God take pleasure in bruising Christ (Isa. 53:10). He smelled a "savour" of rest in this sacrifice. The meaning is that as people are offended with a stench, and their stomachs rise at it, and on the contrary delighted with sweet odors and fragrances, so the blessed God (figuratively speaking) is offended and filled with loathing and abhorrence by our sins but infinitely pleased and delighted in the offering of Christ for them. It went up a "sweetsmelling savour" to Him.

Christ's Presentation

Christ brings this oblation before God and offers it to Him (Heb. 9:14). As Christ assumed the capacity of a surety, so God assumed the capacity of a creditor. He exacted satisfaction from Christ; that is, He required from Him, as our surety, the penalty due to us for our sin. And so, Christ had to deal immediately with a God infinitely wronged and incensed against us on account of our sin. Christ, our High Priest, approached Him, as to a devouring fire, with the sacrifice.

Christ's People

Christ offered Himself to God on behalf of the whole number of the elect—those whom the Father had given Him (John 10:15; 11:50–52; Acts 20:28). It is confessed that there is sufficiency of virtue in this sacrifice to redeem the whole world, and on that account some divines affirm that He is called the "Saviour of the world" (John 4:42). We also acknowledge that the elect are scattered in all parts and among all ranks of people in the world and are unknown to those who are to offer Christ by the preaching of the gospel. Thus, the style of the gospel is by such indefinite expressions suited to the general offers they are to make of Him. But the efficacy and saving virtue of this all-sufficient sacrifice is coextended with God's election so that they alone will reap its special benefits (John 17:2, 9, 19–20; 10:26–28; Eph. 5:23; 1 Tim. 4:10).

Christ's Purpose

The design and end of this oblation was to atone, pacify, and reconcile God, by giving Him a full and adequate compensation (or satisfaction) for the sins of His elect (Col. 1:20). "God was in Christ, reconciling the world unto himself" (2 Cor. 5:19). Reconciliation is the making up of that breach caused by sin between God and us, and the restoring us again to His favor and friendship. This is why Christ offered up Himself to God.

The reconciliation was not only made between us and God the Father. We were reconciled by the blood of the cross to the whole Trinity. Every sin is against the divine Majesty; therefore, the three persons (having the same divine essence) must be offended by it. Likewise, the three persons are reconciled by the expiation and remission of the sin. But reconciliation is said to be with the Father because (though the works of the Trinity are undivided, and what one does all do, and what is done to one is done to all) by this form and manner of expression the Scriptures point out the proper office of each person. The Father receives us into favor; the Son mediates and gives the ransom that procures it; and the Holy Spirit applies and seals this to the persons and hearts of believers. However, being reconciled to the Father, we are also reconciled to the Son and the Spirit, as they are one God in three persons.

Application

Lesson 1

Believers are freed from the guilt of their sins, and they will never come under condemnation. The obligation of sin is perfectly abolished by the virtue of Christ's sacrifice. When He became our sacrifice, He bore away our sins. They were first laid upon Him and then expiated by Him (John 1:29; Heb. 9:26). How great a mercy is this? "And by him all that believe are justified from all things, from which ye could not be justified by the law of Moses" (Acts 13:39). "Blessed is he whose transgression is forgiven, whose sin is covered" (Ps. 32:1). Who can express the comfort and happiness of such a state as this? The blood of Christ "cleanseth us from all sin" (1 John 1:7)—past and present, without exception. Some divines affirm that it also refers to all future sins. I think most agree that our past sins are pardoned without revocation, and that our present sins are pardoned without exception, while there is pardon for our future sins, which is applied upon our repentance and application of Christ's blood. O let these things slide sweetly into our melting hearts!

Lesson 2

Divine justice could be diverted from us in no other way. If Christ had not presented Himself to God for us, justice would not have spared us. And if He appears before God as our surety, it will not spare Him (Rom. 8:32). God spared not His own Son. Sparing mercy is the lowest degree of mercy, yet it was denied to Christ. He did not abate Him a minute of the time appointed for His suffering, nor one degree of the wrath He was to bear. Christ fell upon the ground in the garden, sweat drops of blood, and in that unparalleled agony uttered that pitiful cry, "Father, if it be possible, let this cup pass," and though He broke out upon the cross in that heartrending complaint, "My God, my God, why hast thou forsaken me?" yet there was no abatement. Justice will not bend in the least.

If this is so, what is the case of those who have no interest in Christ's sacrifice? How can they imagine that they can support the infinite wrath of God, which Christ faced in the place of God's elect? He had the strength of God to support Him (Isa. 42:1). He had the fullness of His Spirit to prepare Him (Isa. 61:11). He had the ministry of an angel who came from heaven to relieve Him in His agony (Luke 22:43). He had the ear of His Father to hear Him (Heb. 5:7). He was assured of the victory before the combat (Isa. 50:8). Yet, for all this, He was sorrowful even to death, and His heart melted like wax in the midst of His bowels. If the case stood thus with Christ, notwithstanding all these advantages, how do unbelievers think they will contend with a devouring fire? Woe to those who meet a just and righteous God without a mediator!

Whoever you are, I beseech you to get an interest in this sacrifice. O it is sweet at all times, especially at death, to see the reconciled face of God through Christ and to hear the voice of peace through the blood of the cross!

Lesson 3

Let us labor to get our hearts duly affected with a sight of Christ's oblation to God for us. Whatever our condition or complaint, beholding the Lamb of God who takes away the sin of the world will give us strong support and sweet relief. Do we complain of the hardness of our heart and lack of love for Christ? We must see Him as offered up to God for us. Such a sight will melt our hard heart (Zech. 12:10). Surely, we can never make light of that which lay so heavy upon Christ's soul and body.

Is our heart pressed down to despondency under the guilt of sin so that we think our sin is greater than can be forgiven? "Behold the Lamb of God, which taketh away the sin of the world" (John 1:29). We must remember that no sin can stand before the efficacy of His blood (1 John 1:7). This sacrifice makes full satisfaction unto God. Are we staggering through unbelief? We must see all ratified and established in the blood of the cross (Heb. 9:17–19). Do we find our hearts impatient and disquieted under every cross and trial? We must see how quietly Christ came to the altar, how meekly and patiently He stood under the wrath of God. This will silence and convince us.

In a word, we must strive to see by faith the grace of God and love of Christ in providing and becoming a sacrifice for us. We will see God taking vengeance against sin but sparing the sinner. We will see Christ standing as the body of sin alone, for He was made sin for us, that we might be made the righteousness of God in Him. Blessed be God for Jesus Christ!

13

The Priest's Intercession

Wherefore he is able also to save them to the uttermost that come unto God by him, seeing he ever liveth to make intercession for them.
—HEBREWS 7:25

Having considered the first act of Christ's priesthood, His oblation, we come to the second act, His intercession. It is the virtual continuation of His offering—the way and means of applying to us the benefits purchased by it. This second act of His priesthood was typified by the high priest's entrance with the blood of the sacrifice and sweet incense into the holy place (Lev. 16:12–14). Christ's offering of Himself on earth corresponded to the killing of the sacrifice outside the holy place, while His entering into heaven to intercede corresponded to the high priest's going with blood and incense within the veil.

This part of Christ's priesthood was so necessary that if He had not done this, all His work on earth would have signified nothing. He would not have been a complete and perfect priest if He had remained on earth (Heb. 8:4). The very design and purpose of shedding His blood on earth would have been frustrated if He had not carried it into heaven. He acted the first part of His priesthood on earth in a state of deep abasement in the form of a servant, but He acts this second part in glory so that He may fulfill His design in dying.

The words in our verse contain an encouragement to believers to come to God in the way of faith. It is drawn from Christ's intercession in heaven for us. We may take note of these principal parts.

First, the quality of the persons who are encouraged: they "come unto God by him." They are described by a direct act of faith. Conscious of great unworthiness in themselves, and apt to be discouraged, they go out of themselves to God by faith.

Second, the encouragement propounded to such believers: "he is able to save them to the uttermost." They go to the Father in Christ's name, and He saves them to "the uttermost"—fully, perfectly, completely.

Third, the ground (or reason) of Christ's saving ability: "he ever liveth to make intercession for them." He has not only offered up His blood to God upon the cross as a full price to purchase grace and pardon for believers, but He lives in heaven to apply unto us (in the way of intercession) all the fruits, blessings, and benefits that His precious blood deserves.

Doctrine: Christ, our High Priest, lives forever in heaven, in the capacity of an intercessor for believers.

In general, to intercede is to go between two parties, to entreat and plead with one for the other. There are two sorts: (1) when a Christian prays and pleads with God for others (1 Tim. 2:1–2) and (2) when Christ presents Himself before God to request for us. The first is performed in another's name. We cannot tender a request to God immediately. The second is proper to Christ. It is an intercession with God for us, in His own name and upon account of His own merit. The one is a private act of charity, while the other is a public act of office. And so, Christ is our advocate who pleads for us and continues peace and friendship between God and us (1 John 2:1–2).

Thus, to make intercession is Christ's peculiar and incommunicable prerogative. He alone can go in His own name to God (Ezek. 44:2–3). We must come to God by virtue of the Mediator and through the benefit of His death imputed to us.

The Work of Christ's Intercession

Christ's intercession includes three acts. First, Christ presents Himself before God in our names and upon our account (Heb. 9:28). In the Old Testament, the high priest appeared in the holy of holies, which was a figure of heaven, and presented to God the names of the twelve tribes of Israel, which were on his breast and shoulders (Ex. 28:9–29). The very sight of Christ, our High Priest, in heaven prevails exceedingly with God and turns away His displeasure from us. When God looks upon the rainbow, which is the sign of the covenant, He remembers the earth in mercy. Likewise, when He looks on Christ, His heart is moved toward us upon Christ's account.

Second, Christ performs His work of intercession in heaven, not only by appearing in the presence of God but by presenting His blood and all His sufferings to God. An interceding voice is attributed to His blood. It is said to speak "better things than that of Abel" (Heb. 12:24). It cries out efficaciously (Rev. 5:9). The wounds He received for our sins are (as it were) still bleeding in heaven. They are a moving and prevailing argument with the Father to give what Christ asks.

Third, Christ presents the prayers of His saints with His merits to God, and He desires that they may be granted for His sake. He causes a cloud of incense to ascend before God. All of this was typified by the high priest going before the Lord with the names of the children of Israel on his breast, with the blood of the sacrifice, and with his hands full of incense (Heb. 7, 9).

The Efficacy of Christ's Intercession

Christ's intercession is successful and prevalent with God for two reasons. First, Christ is fit in every way for the work in which He is engaged. Whatever is desirable in an advocate is in Him. It is necessary that he who pleads the cause of another should be wise, faithful, tenderhearted, and personally concerned in the success of his business. Our advocate, Christ, lacks no wisdom to manage His work. He is "the only wise God" (Jude 25). He is also faithful; therefore, He is called a "faithful high priest in things pertaining to God" (Heb. 2:17). He assures us that we may safely entrust our concerns to Him. For tenderheartedness, there is none like Him: "For we have not an high priest which cannot be touched with the feeling of our infirmities; but was in all points tempted like as we are, yet without sin" (Heb. 4:15). That He might the better sympathize with us, He came as near to our condition as the holiness of His nature permitted. And then, for His concernment in the success of His work, He really made it His own interest. By reason of the mystical union, all our wants and troubles are His; yea, His own glory and completeness, as mediator, is deeply interested in it (Eph. 1:23). Therefore, we need not doubt that He will use all care and diligence in His work. In addition to this, consider the great interest He has in the Father, with whom He intercedes. Christ is His dear Son (Col. 1:13) and His beloved Son (Eph. 1:6). Between Him and the Father there is a unity, not only of nature but of will, so as He always hears Him (John 11:42). We must remember that the Father is under a bond and covenant to do what His Son asks.

Second, Christ's intercession is prevalent with God because of our relation to Him. We are the friends of God, the children of God, and the object of God's love. It must be so, for the first cornerstone of all these mercies was laid by the Father in His free election of us. He also delivered His Son for us, and "how shall he not with him also freely give us all things?" (Rom. 8:32). So then, there can remain no doubt that Christ is a prevalent and successful intercessor in heaven.

The Eternality of Christ's Intercession

Christ lives forever in heaven to make intercession. In what sense are we perfect in heaven if we still need Christ's intercession? By way of an answer, we must distinguish between the essence (or substance) of Christ's offices and the way (or manner) of their administration. In the first sense, Christ's intercession is eternal, for His mediatory kingdom (as to the essence of it) abides forever. Christ will never cease to be a mediator. However, when He has accomplished the design for which He became a mediator, He will deliver up the kingdom to the Father (1 Cor. 15:24). Then, the divinity of Christ, which was so emptied and obscured in the undertaking of His mediatorship, will be more gloriously manifested by the full possession and enjoyment of that natural, divine, eternal kingdom, which belongs to all the three coessential and coequal persons, reigning with the same power, majesty, and glory, in the unity of the divine essence, and common acts, in all and over all, infinitely and immutably forever.

And so, Christ continues as our Mediator forever. But this does not imply that our happiness will be incomplete, but that the church will no longer be governed as it is now. It will be ruled more immediately, gloriously, triumphantly, and ineffably in the world to come. The substance of His mediatorship will not be changed, but the manner of its administration.

Application
Lesson 1
The condition of those who have no interest in Christ's blood is lamentable. Instead of pleading for them, Christ's blood cries out to God against them. Every unbeliever despises it. The apostate even treads it under foot. To be guilty of a man's blood is sad, but to have the blood of Christ accusing and crying to God against a person is unspeakably terrible. What do men and women do in rejecting Christ's gracious offer? They tread upon a savior, cast contempt by unbelief and hardness of heart upon their only remedy. Does not Christ smile upon us in the gospel? And will you (as it were) stab Him in the heart with your infidelity? Woe to that man against whom this blood cries in heaven!

Lesson 2
We can derive, from Christ's intercession, relief and encouragement for all our fears and troubles. Surely, it answers them

all. First, we are encouraged against our sinful infirmities and weaknesses. These grieve the Spirit of God, sadden our hearts, and cloud our evidences, but "we have an advocate with the Father, Jesus Christ the righteous" (1 John 2:1). He stops whatever charge the law or the devil might bring against us. He answers it all by His satisfaction. He gets out fresh pardons for new sins. When we are cast down under the sense of sin, we must remember that Christ is able to save to the uttermost.

Second, we are encouraged against our lifeless prayers. At times, we complain that our hearts are dead, wandering, and distracted in duty. We must remember that Christ's blood speaks when we cannot. It pleads for us when we are unable to speak for ourselves.

Third, we are encouraged against our slavish fears. Christ's intercession promotes the fear of reverence, suppresses unbelieving despondencies, and destroys the spirit of bondage (Heb. 10:19–22). We can come to God as a ship comes with full sail into the harbor. O what a full and direct gale of encouragement does Christ's intercession give to the poor soul!

Fourth, we are encouraged against the fears of deserting Christ by apostasy. This is how Christ relieved Peter. "Simon, Simon, behold, Satan hath desired to have you, that he may sift you as wheat: but I have prayed for thee, that thy faith fail not" (Luke 22:31–32). Satan's temptations are aimed at our faith, but we have no need to fear, for Christ's prayer will break his designs and secure our faith against all his attacks. Christ's powerful intercession keeps us against all that threatens to bring us into a state of condemnation (Rom. 8:34–35).

Fifth, we are encouraged against the defects in our sanctification. We lack a great deal of faith, love, heavenly mindedness, mortification, and knowledge. But, if grace is in its infancy in our soul, we may be encouraged that, by reason of Christ's intercession, it will grow. He is not only the author of it but the finisher of it (Heb. 12:2). He is always requesting new and fresh mercies for us in heaven, and He will never cease until all our wants are supplied.

Lesson 3

We are encouraged to pursue constancy in the good ways of God. We must "hold fast our profession" (Heb. 4:14). He has passed into the heavens as our Great High Priest to intercede; therefore, we cannot miscarry. This should encourage us to be constant in prayer. We must not neglect this excellent duty, seeing Christ is in heaven to present all our petitions to God (Heb. 4:16).

14

A Full Satisfaction

Christ hath redeemed us from the curse of the law, being made a curse for us.
—GALATIANS 3:13

We have considered the nature, necessity, and parts (oblation and intercession) of Christ's priesthood. Before we leave His priestly office, it is important to consider its principal fruits and effects. The first is a full satisfaction. It is affirmed in the verse before us. Previously, the apostle declared, "Cursed is every one that continucth not in all things which are written in the book of the law to do them" (v. 10). Now he declares, "Christ hath redeemed us from the curse of the law, being made a curse for us." This verse affirms two truths.

First, our deliverance: "Christ hath redeemed us from the curse of the law." God's law has three parts: commands, promises, and curses. The curse of the law is its condemning sentence, whereby sinners are bound over to death. The chain by which it binds them is the guilt of sin. This curse of the law is the most dreadful thing imaginable. It strikes at the life of a sinner, yea, the eternal life of the soul. When it has condemned, it is unchangeable. No cries, no tears, no reformation, no repentance can free the guilty sinner. It requires what no mere creature can give—infinite satisfaction. Christ alone frees believers from this curse. He dissolves the obligation to punishment and breaks all the bonds and chains of guilt, so that the curse of the law has nothing to do with us.

Second, the means of our deliverance: "being made a curse for us." Christ redeems us by making a full payment—complete satisfaction. He pays a price that is in every way adequate and proportionate to the wrong. This price is a ransom (Matt. 20:28; 1 Tim. 2:5–6; Rev. 5:9). As the ransom was full, perfect, and sufficient, so it was paid in our place and upon our account. He was "made a curse for us." This does not mean that Christ was made the very curse itself (i.e., changed into a curse), but that Christ took the curse upon Himself (2 Cor. 5:21).

Doctrine: Christ's death has made a full satisfaction to God for all the sins of His elect.

"He was oppressed, and he was afflicted" (Isa. 53:7). Here we read of Christ's satisfaction. "In whom we have redemption through his blood, even the forgiveness of sins" (Col. 1:14). Here we read of the benefit of Christ's satisfaction ("redemption…even the forgiveness of sins") and the matchless price that purchased it ("his blood"). "By his own blood he entered in once into the holy place, having obtained eternal redemption for us" (Heb. 9:12). Again, here we read of the benefit of Christ's satisfaction ("eternal redemption") and the price that procured it ("his own blood").

Because the doctrine of Christ's satisfaction is so weighty, and yet so opposed and maligned by numerous enemies, I will take the time to explain it in more detail.

The Nature of Christ's Satisfaction

Christ's satisfaction is the act by which He presents Himself as our surety, in obedience to God and out of love for us, to do and suffer all that the law required of us, thereby freeing us from the wrath and curse due to us for our sins.

First, it is the act of the God-man. No one else was capable of giving satisfaction for an infinite wrong done to God. By reason of the union of the two natures in His wonderful person, He could do it, and He has done it for us. The human nature did what was necessary in its kind; it gave the matter of the sacrifice. The divine nature stamped the value and dignity upon it, which made it an adequate compensation. It was the act of the God-man, yet so that each nature retained its own properties, notwithstanding their joint influence into the effect. If all the angels in heaven had laid down their lives, or if all the people on earth had poured out their blood, it could never have satisfied. It was God who redeemed the church with His own blood (Acts 20:28).

Second, having satisfied God for us, Christ presents Himself before God as our surety in our place as well as for our good. To this end, He was "made under the law" (Gal. 4:4)—that is, under the same obligation with us as a surety (Heb. 7:22). Indeed, His obedience and suffering could not be exacted from Him on any other account. It was not for anything He had done that He became a curse. It was prophesied that He would be "cut off, but not for himself" (Dan. 9:26; see also

Matt. 20:28; Rom. 4:25; 1 Cor. 15:3; Heb. 10:12; 1 Peter 3:18). This consideration supports the doctrine of imputation—the imputation of our sin to Christ, and the imputation of Christ's righteousness to us (Rom. 5:19). How could our sins be laid on Him unless He stood in our place? And how can His righteousness be imputed to us unless He was our surety, acting in our place? To deny Christ's suffering in our stead is to lose the cornerstone of our justification and overthrow the very pillar that supports our faith, comfort, and salvation.

Third, the internal moving cause of Christ's satisfaction for us was His obedience to God and love for us. He "became obedient unto death, even the death of the cross" (Phil. 2:8). Now obedience respects a command, and such a command Christ received: "I lay [my life] down of myself. I have power to lay it down, and I have power to take it again. This commandment have I received of my Father" (John 10:18). It was an act of obedience with respect to God and yet a most free and spontaneous act with respect to Himself. He was moved to it out of pity and love to us. As the apostle Paul sweetly reflects, Christ "loved me" and "gave himself for me" (Gal. 2:20). As the external moving cause was our misery, so the internal moving cause was His own love and pity for us.

Fourth, the matter of Christ's satisfaction was His active and passive obedience to all that God's law required. It is true that the Scriptures most frequently mention His passive obedience as that which makes atonement and procures redemption (Matt. 20:28; 26:28; Rom. 4:24–25). But His passive obedience is implied in other Scriptures. He was "made under the law, to redeem them that were under the law" (Gal. 4:4–5). Being "made under the law" cannot be restricted to

His subjection to the law's curse but also includes its commands. "For as by one man's disobedience many were made sinners, so by the obedience of one shall many be made righteous" (Rom. 5:19). It would be a manifest injury to this text to limit it to Christ's passive obedience. In short, this twofold obedience of Christ stands opposed to a twofold obligation that fallen man is under—the one to do what God requires and the other to suffer what He has threatened for disobedience. We owe Him active obedience as His creatures and passive obedience as His prisoners. Corresponding to this double obligation, Christ comes under the commandment of the law to fulfill it actively (Matt. 3:15) and under the curse of the law to satisfy it passively. Both of these make up that one, entire, and complete obedience by which God is satisfied and we are justified.

Fifth, the effect and fruit of Christ's satisfaction is our freedom, ransom, or deliverance from the wrath and curse due to us for our sins. Such was the dignity, value, and completeness of Christ's satisfaction that in strict justice it merited our full redemption and deliverance. If He is made a curse for us, then we must be redeemed from the curse according to justice (Rom. 3:25–26). God's design in exacting satisfaction from Christ was to declare His righteousness in the remission of sin to believers. Everyone can see how His mercy is declared in remission. But He would have us take notice that His justification of believers is an act of justice and that He, as a just God, cannot condemn believers since Christ has satisfied their debt. This attribute seems to be the main bar against remission, but now it has become the very ground and reason why God remits. O how comfortable a text this is! God has set forth Christ to be a propitiation. Justice is manifested, satisfied, and glorified in His death.

The Defense of Christ's Satisfaction

We will gather up all that has been said to establish the truth of Christ's satisfaction. It is not fictitious, as some have called it. It is full, real, and proper, and as such accepted by God. For His blood is the blood of a surety (Heb. 7:22). He came under the same obligations of the law as us (Gal. 4:4), and though He had no sin of His own, yet, standing before God as our surety, our iniquities were laid on Him (Isa. 53:6). God exacted satisfaction from Him for our sins (Rom. 8:32). He punished them upon His soul (Matt. 27:46) and body (Acts 2:23). He is fully pleased and satisfied with His Son's obedience (Eph. 5:2), and He has in token thereof raised Him from the dead and set Him at His own right hand (1 Tim. 3:16). On account of Christ's righteousness, God acquits and discharges believers, who will never come into condemnation (Rom. 8:1, 34).

All this is plain in Scripture. Our faith in Christ's satisfaction is not built on human wisdom, but the everlasting sealed truth of God. Yet such is the perverse nature of man and the pride of his heart that, while he should humbly adore God's grace in providing such a surety for us, he is found accusing God's justice and diminishing God's mercy, and raising all the objections that Satan and his own heart can invent, to overturn that blessed foundation upon which God has built His own honor and His people's salvation.

We reject with deep abhorrence that doctrine which ascribes to us any power, in whole or in part, to satisfy God for our sins or other people's sins. No creature can do this by active obedience. With similar detestation, we reject that doctrine which makes the satisfaction of Christ impossible, or fictitious, or inconsistent with grace in the free pardon of sin. Many are the objections raised against Christ's satisfaction. The principal are the following.

Objection 1. If Christ satisfied God by paying our debt, then (since Christ is God) God satisfied Himself. *Answer.* God cannot properly be said to satisfy Himself, for that would be the same thing as to pardon without any satisfaction. But there is a twofold consideration of Christ. (1) In respect of His essence and divine nature, He is the object both of the offense and of the satisfaction made for it. (2) In respect of His person and office, He satisfies God, being in respect of His manhood inferior to God (John 14:28). The blood of the man, Christ Jesus, is the matter of the satisfaction; the divine nature dignifies it and makes it of infinite value.

Objection 2. If Christ satisfied God by paying our debt, then He should have endured eternal torment. *Answer.* We must distinguish between what is essential and what is accidental in punishment. The primary intent of the law is reparation and satisfaction. He who can make it at one entire payment (as Christ could and did) ought to be discharged. He who cannot (as no mere creature can) ought to be under sufferings eternally.

Objection 3. If Christ satisfied God by paying our debt, then God is satisfied for our sins before He pardons them. *Answer.* Pardon could not be an act of pure grace if God received satisfaction from us; but if He pardons us upon the satisfaction received from Christ, though it is of debt to Him, it is of grace to us. For it was grace to admit a surety to satisfy, more grace to provide Him, and most of all to apply His satisfaction to us by uniting us to Christ, as He has done.

Objection 4. If Christ satisfied God by paying our debt, then God loved us before Christ died for us, for it was the love of God for the world that moved Him to give His only begotten Son. Could God love us and yet not be reconciled to us? *Answer.* God's complacent love is indeed inconsistent with an unreconciled state. He is reconciled to everyone He so loves. But His benevolent love, consisting in His purpose of good, may be before actual reconciliation and satisfaction.

Objection 5. If Christ satisfied God by paying our debt, then why do we die? Temporal death, as well as eternal death, is a part of the curse. *Answer.* Temporal death is a penal evil and part of the curse, and so God does not inflict it upon believers. We die for other reasons—namely, to be made perfectly happy in a more full and immediate enjoyment of God than we can enjoy in the body. And so, death is ours by way of privilege. Our death is not by way of punishment. The same may be said of all the afflictions that God, for gracious ends, brings upon His reconciled ones.

Application
Lesson 1
There is an infinite evil in sin since it cannot be expiated but by an infinite satisfaction. Fools make a mockery of sin, and

there are only a few people in the world who are duly affected by its evil. If God should damn us for all eternity, our eternal suffering could not satisfy for the evil that is in one vain thought. Perhaps someone thinks this is harsh and severe, but when we consider that the object against whom we sin is the infinite and blessed God, we think otherwise. O the depth of sin's evil! If we will ever see how great and horrid sin is, we must measure it in our thoughts by the infinite holiness and excellence of God who is wronged by it, or by the infinite suffering of Christ who died to satisfy for it. Then we will have a deeper apprehension of the evil of sin.

Lesson 2
The redemption of souls is costly. "Forasmuch as ye know that ye were not redeemed with corruptible things, as silver and gold, from your vain conversation received by tradition from your fathers; but with the precious blood of Christ, as of a lamb without blemish and without spot" (1 Peter 1:18–19). Souls are of great value to God. He who paid for them found them to be so. Yet sinners sell their souls as if they were but cheap commodities.

Lesson 3
Christ's love for poor sinners is unparalleled. He did not share in the penalty with us; He bore it all. He did it for enemies who were fighting and rebelling against Him (Rom. 5:8).

Lesson 4
God is no loser in pardoning the greatest sinners who believe in Christ. Consequently, His justice can be no impediment

to our justification and salvation. He is just to forgive us our sins (1 John 1:9). What an argument is here for a poor believer to plead with God! One drop of Christ's blood is worth more than all our polluted blood. O this is satisfying to the consciences of poor sinners who are overwhelmed by their sins! Can such a sinner as I be forgiven? Yes, if we believe in Christ. For God will lose nothing in pardoning the greatest transgressors. "Let Israel hope in the LORD: for with the LORD there is mercy, and with him is plenteous redemption" (Ps. 130:7).

Lesson 5
We must abandon all thoughts of satisfying God for our sins and turn ourselves to Christ's blood, that we may be pardoned. It grieves my heart to see how many people look to their repentance, reformation, and obedience to satisfy God for what they have done against Him. If they could weep until they can weep no more and cry until their throats are parched, they could never recompence God for one vain thought. Such is the severity of the law that, when it is once offended, it will never be made right by anything that we can do. It will not discharge the sinner for all the sorrow in the world. Indeed, if we are in Christ, then sorrow for sin is something and renewed obedience is something; God looks upon them favorably and accepts them graciously. But, outside of Christ, they signify nothing more than the cries of a condemned malefactor to reverse the legal sentence of the judge. One act of faith in Christ pleases God more than all our obedience and repentance.

15

A Blessed Inheritance

But when the fulness of time was come, God sent forth his Son, made of a woman, made under the law, to redeem them that were under the law, that we might receive the adoption of sons.
—GALATIANS 4:4–5

These verses describe the twofold fruit of Christ's death. The first is the payment of our debt: "to redeem them that were under the law." We considered this in the last sermon. The second is the purchase of our inheritance: "the adoption of sons." Adoption is either civil or divine. Civil adoption is a lawful act, invented for the comfort of those who have no children of their own. Divine adoption is that special benefit whereby God, for Christ's sake, accepts us as sons and makes us heirs of eternal life with Him.

There is a twofold agreement and disagreement between civil and divine adoption. They agree in that (1) both flow from the pleasure and goodwill of the adoptee and (2) both confer a right to privileges which we do not have by nature. They differ in that (1) one imitates nature, while the other transcends nature and (2) one exists for the comfort of those who have no children, while the other exists for the comfort of those who have no father. Divine adoption is, in Scripture, either taken properly for the act (or sentence) of God by which we are made sons or for the privileges with which the adopted are invested. It is used in this second sense in our verse. We lost our inheritance by Adam's fall. We receive it by Christ's death, which restores it to us by a new and better title.

Doctrine: Christ's death has not only satisfied for our debts but has purchased a rich inheritance for us.

Christ is the Mediator of the New Testament, so that by means of His death we might receive the promise of the eternal inheritance.

What Christ Paid

Christ's obedience has a double relation: (1) a price that is proportionate to the law and (2) a merit that far exceeds the law. This surplus of satisfaction (which was the price of our inheritance) is plainly expressed in Romans 5. "But not as the offence, so also is the free gift. For if through the offence of one many be dead, much more the grace of God, and the gift by grace, which is by one man, Jesus Christ, hath abounded unto many" (v. 15). "For if by one man's offence death reigned by one; much more they which receive abundance of grace and of the gift of righteousness shall reign in life by one, Jesus Christ" (v. 17).

In both places, Christ and Adam are compared as the two roots (or common heads) of humanity, both agreeing in this property of communicating their conditions to those who are theirs. Yet there is a great difference between them. In Christ the power is all divine and therefore infinitely more active and effectual. He communicates abundantly more to His people than what they lost in Adam. His blood is not only sufficient to redeem all those who are actually redeemed by it, but even the whole world. His blood is infinite in its worth and dignity. Therefore, the superabundance of merit is great indeed.

Our divines rightly distinguish between the substance and accidents of Christ's death and obedience. As to the substance of it, it was no more than what the law required. As to the circumstances of it, the person of the sufferer and the cause and efficacy of His suffering, it was much more than sufficient—a merit above and beyond what the law required. Though the law required the death of the sinner, who is but a poor contemptible creature, it did not require that one perfectly innocent should die. It did not require that God should shed His blood. It did not require blood of such value and worth as Christ's was. God was pleased for the advancement and manifestation of His justice and mercy in the highest to admit and order this by way of commutation. Hereby we are not only redeemed from wrath by the adequate compensation made for our sins by Christ's blood and suffering, substantially considered, but we are entitled to a most glorious inheritance, purchased by His blood, considered as the blood of an innocent, as the blood of God, and therefore as most excellent and efficacious blood, above what the law demanded.

By this we see how rich a treasure lies in Christ, to bestow in a purchase for us above what He paid to redeem us, even as much as His soul and body were worth more than ours. It is so great a sum that all the angels in heaven and humans on earth can never compute so as to show the total of it. This was the inexhaustible treasure that Christ expended to procure and purchase the fairest inheritance for believers.

What Christ Purchased

This inheritance is so large that it cannot be surveyed by creatures, nor can its boundaries and limits be described, for it comprehends all things (1 Cor. 3:22; Rev. 21:7). By His death, Christ has restored a right to all things to His people. To be more particular, this inheritance includes the following.

First, it includes all temporal good things (1 Tim. 4:4). We do not possess all things, but the comfort and benefit of all things (2 Cor. 6:10). We use the world and enjoy God in the use of it. But unbelievers are deceived, defiled, and destroyed by the world.

Second, it includes all spiritual good things (1 Cor. 1:30): justification, sanctification (initial and progressive), and adoption. The very faith, which is the bond of union between Christ and us, and consequently the ground of all our communion with Christ, is also the purchase of His blood (2 Peter 1:1). This most precious grace is the dear purchase of our Lord Jesus Christ; yea, all the peace, joy, and comfort, which are sweet fruits of faith, are purchased with it for us by His blood (Rom. 5:1–3). Moreover, the Holy Spirit Himself, who is the author, fountain, and spring of all graces and comforts, is procured for us by Christ's death and resurrection (Gal. 3:13–14). The Holy Spirit, who sanctifies, seals, comforts, directs, guides, and quickens our souls, would not perform any of these blessed offices upon our hearts unless Christ had died for us.

Third, it includes all eternal good things. Heaven, and all its glory, is purchased for us with this price. Hence, it is called "an inheritance incorruptible, and undefiled, and that fadeth not away, reserved in heaven for you" (1 Peter 1:4). We were "begotten" to this "lively hope by the resurrection of Jesus Christ from the dead" (v. 3). We are prudent and prospecting creatures who are not satisfied that it is well with us for the present unless we have some assurance it will be well with us in the future. Our minds are taken up with what will be, and we experience vast hopes or fears from the good or evil things to come. Therefore, to complete our happiness, and fill up the uttermost capacity of our souls, all the good of eternity is put into the account and inventory of our estate and inheritance. This happiness is inexpressible. It consists of the following.

First, objective happiness, which is God Himself (Ps. 73:25). It is no heaven for us unless God is there. Our glory in heaven is to be with God forever (1 Thess. 4:17). God Himself is the chief part of our inheritance, in which sense (as some understand it) we are called "heirs of God" (Rom. 8:17).

Second, subjective happiness, which is the suiting of our soul and body to God. This is begun in sanctification and perfected in glorification. It consists of (1) removing all that is indecent and inconsistent with a state of such complete glory and happiness and (2) clothing it with all heavenly qualities. Our bodies will be freed from all infirmities. There will be no diseases, deformities, pains, or flaws. They will be made like Christ's glorious body (1 Cor. 15:44; Phil. 3:21). Our souls will be freed from all darkness and ignorance of mind and will be able to discern all truths in God. The memory's leaks will be stopped forever. The imagination's roving will be perfectly cured. The will's stubbornness will be subdued in full subjection to God. In sum, the saints in glory will be free from all that now troubles them. We will never sin again, nor ever be tempted to do so. We will never grieve nor groan again, for God will wipe away all tears from our eyes. We will never be troubled again, for God will recompense us with rest. We will never doubt again, for fruition excludes doubting.

Third, formal happiness, which is the fullness of satisfaction resulting from the blessed sight and enjoyment of God. "I shall be satisfied, when I awake, with thy likeness" (Ps. 17:15). This sight of God in glory, called the beatific vision, yields inexpressible satisfaction to the soul. The intellectual (or mental) eye will see God (1 John 3:2). The corporeal eye will see Christ (Job 19:26–27). What a ravishing vision this will be! It will be a *transformative* vision; it will change us into its own image and likeness (1 John 3:2). As iron put into the fire becomes all fiery, so the soul by conversing with God is changed into His very similitude. It will be an *appropriative* vision; our interest in God will be clear and without doubt. It will be an *eternal* vision; we will enjoy it forever, without any diversion or distraction. It will be a *satisfying* vision; God will be all in all. The blessed soul will feel itself filled and satisfied in every part. O what a happiness is here! To look, love, drink, and sing at the fountainhead of the highest glory!

All this is purchased for believers; hence it is called "the inheritance of the saints in light" (Col. 1:12; see also Luke 12:32; Rom. 8:17, 30; 1 Cor. 3:23; 6:9).

Application
Lesson 1
We should be content with God's providence in this life. O let not such things as grumbling, repining, and fretting be found (or even named) among those who share in this great inheritance! Suppose you were to adopt a beggar as your son and make him the heir of a large inheritance, and after this he quarrels with you over a trifle—would you bear it? We must learn to cultivate a spirit of contentment while in a low condition here.

Lesson 2
We should walk with weaned affections, content with life or death (Phil. 1:23–24). Present things are ours while we live, and future things are ours when we die. Who can be blamed for desiring to see that fair inheritance which is purchased for us? We should be ready to pull down the prison walls and have patience to wait until God opens the door. "And the Lord direct your hearts into the love of God, and into the patient waiting for Christ" (2 Thess. 3:5). Love inflames with desire, while patience allays that fervor. Thus, fervent desires are allayed with meek submission, and mighty love with strong patience.

Lesson 3
We infer the impossibility of the salvation of those who do not know Christ nor have an interest in His blood. Scripture knows no other way to glory but through Christ. He must be applied by faith. No one, by the sole conduct of nature, without the knowledge of Christ, can be saved. There is but one way to glory for all the world (John 14:6). Scripture asserts

the impossibility of being or doing anything that is truly evangelically good, outside of Christ (John 15:5; Heb. 11:6). Scripture chains salvation with vocation, and vocation with the gospel (Rom. 8:30; 10:14).

Lesson 4

We should clear up our title to this heavenly inheritance. It is horrible to see how industrious many are for an inheritance on earth and how careless they are for heaven. By this we plainly see how much the noble soul is depressed by sin, minding only the concernments of the flesh. Hear me, you who labor for the world as if heaven were in it! What will you do when, at death, you look back over your shoulder and see all that you have spent your time and strength for, shrinking and vanishing away? What will you do when you look forward and see a vast eternity opening its mouth to swallow you? If you have any concern for your poor soul, "give diligence to make your calling and election sure" (2 Peter 1:10). "Work out your own salvation with fear and trembling. For it is God which worketh in you both to will and to do of his good pleasure" (Phil. 2:12). God offers you His helping hand. The Holy Spirit waits upon you in the means. But you do not know how long this will last. You must get to work.

If we have solid evidence that the inheritance is ours, we should adore God's free grace that has entitled children of wrath to a heavenly inheritance. We should walk as becomes heirs of God and joint heirs with Christ. When we feel pinches here, we should look heavenward—to that fair estate that is reserved in heaven for us. We must consider what it cost Christ to purchase it for us, and let our soul say, "Blessed be God for Jesus Christ!"

16

The King's Spiritual Reign

Casting down imaginations, and every high thing that exalteth itself against the knowledge of God, and bringing into captivity every thought to the obedience of Christ.
—2 CORINTHIANS 10:5

We come to the kingly office by which our glorious Mediator executes the design of our redemption. If He had not (as our prophet) revealed the way of life and salvation to us, we could never have known it. And if we had known it, but He (as our priest) had not offered up Himself for us, we could never have been redeemed virtually by His blood. And if we had been redeemed, but He (as our king) had not applied the purchase of His blood to us, we could have had no actual or personal benefit by His death. What He revealed as a prophet, He purchased as a priest; and what He revealed and purchased as a prophet and priest, He applies as a king.

Christ performs His kingly office by subduing His elect to His spiritual government and by ruling over them as His subjects, ordering all things in the kingdom of providence for their good. This means that Christ has a twofold kingdom:

the first is spiritual and internal, by which He subdues and rules the hearts of His people; and the second is providential and external, whereby He rules, guides, and orders all things in the world in a blessed subordination to the eternal salvation of His people.

Our verse speaks of the first kingdom: the spiritual and internal. The words may be considered in two ways: relatively or absolutely. Considered relatively, they are a vindication of the apostle from the unjust censures of the Corinthians, who interpreted his gentleness and condescension to be no better than a fawning upon them for selfish ends, and his authority to be no better than pride and arrogance. He lets them know that he never used such carnal pretenses. The weapons of our warfare are not carnal, but mighty through God. Considered absolutely, the words declare the efficacy of the gospel, in the plainness and simplicity of it, for the subduing of rebellious sinners to Christ. I want to consider three things.

First, the sinner's opposition to the gospel: "imaginations." By this term, the apostle Paul means the excuses and arguments of carnal people, by which they fortify and entrench themselves against the convictions of the Word. There are many carnal reasonings and proud conceits that overwhelm sinners and make them unwilling to submit to the humble and self-denying way of the gospel. These are the carnal mind's fortifications against Christ.

Second, the gospel's conquest of the sinner: "casting down." Christ spoils Satan of the armor in which he trusted by showing sinners that it can provide no defense against God's wrath.

Third, the improvement of the victory: "bringing into captivity every thought to the obedience of Christ." Christ not only leads away these spoiled enemies, but He brings them into obedience to Himself. After conversion, He makes them subjects of His own kingdom—useful and serviceable to Him. And so, He is more than a conqueror. They not only lay down their arms and cease to fight against Christ, but they join His camp to fight for Him. And so, enemies and rebels are subdued and made subjects of Christ's spiritual kingdom.

Doctrine: Christ exercises a kingly power over all those whom the gospel subdues to His obedience.

As soon as the Colossian believers were delivered out of the power of darkness, they were translated into the kingdom of Christ (Col. 1:13). This is the internal and spiritual kingdom, which is said to be within the saints (Luke 17:20–21). Christ sits as an enthroned king in the hearts, consciences, and affections of His willing people (Ps. 110:3). And His kingdom consists of "righteousness, and peace, and joy in the Holy Ghost" (Rom. 14:17).

The Establishment of Christ's Rule

Christ obtains a throne in people's hearts by conquest. The elect are His by right of donation (the Father gave them to Him) and redemption (He died for them), but Satan has the first possession. The house is conveyed to Christ by Him who built it, but the armed man keeps possession of it until a stronger man comes and ejects him (Luke 11:20–22). Christ must fight His way into the soul, though He has a right to enter. When the time of recovering the elect arrives, He sends forth His armies to subdue them (Ps. 110:3). Christ sent forth His armies of prophets, apostles, evangelists, pastors, and teachers under the conduct of His Spirit, armed with the two-edged sword, the Word of God (Heb. 4:12). But that is not all. He causes armies of convictions to trouble them on every side, so that they do not know what to do. These convictions, like a shower of arrows, strike into their consciences (Acts 2:37). By these convictions He batters down all their vain hopes.

When Christ sits down before the soul, and summons it by His messengers, it is a time of great distress. Satan is so deeply entrenched in the mind and will that the soul does not yield at the first summons. Its towers of carnal pride and walls of vain confidence must be undermined by the gospel. Only then does the soul desire a parley with Christ. It sends messengers to Christ, who has come to its very gates: "Mercy, Lord, mercy!" Now, the merciful King, whose only design is to conquer the heart, waves the white flag of mercy before the soul, giving it hope that it will be pitied and pardoned if it will yield to Him. "Let the wicked forsake his way, and the unrighteous man his thoughts: and let him return unto the LORD, and he will have mercy upon him; and to our God, for he will abundantly pardon" (Isa. 55:7). Encouraged by these messages of grace (Matt. 11:28; John 6:37; Heb. 7:25), the soul resolves to open to Christ. The will submits and yields. And so, the soul is won to Christ. He writes down His terms, and the soul willingly accepts them. Thus, it comes to Christ by free and hearty submission, desiring nothing more than to come under Christ's government.

The Exercise of Christ's Rule

How does Christ rule in those who submit to Him? First, He imposes a new law upon us and requires us to be punctual in our obedience. Formerly, we could not endure any restraint (Titus 3:3). But now we must be under law to Christ. These are the articles of peace that we willingly accept in the day of our admission to mercy. This "law of the Spirit of life in Christ Jesus hath made me free from the law of sin and death" (Rom. 8:2). Here is much strictness, but no bondage, for the law is not only written in Scripture but copied out by His Spirit upon the hearts of His subjects. This makes obedience a pleasure. Christ's yoke is lined with love so that it never wounds the necks of His people. "His commandments are not grievous" (1 John 5:3). Those who come under Christ's government must receive His law.

Second, Christ rebukes and chastises us for the violation and transgression of His law. This is another act of His kingly authority (Heb. 12:6–7). His chastisements are either upon our bodies and outward comforts or upon our souls and inward comforts. The affliction of the inner man is a much harder rod. Christ withdraws peace and takes away joy from the souls of His people. The hiding of His face is a sore rebuke; however, it is for correction, not destruction.

Third, Christ restrains His servants from iniquity. He withholds us from those courses that our own hearts would follow. Our soul is bent to backsliding, but Christ in tenderness keeps us from iniquity by removing the occasion or helping us to resist the temptation (1 Cor. 10:13). We have many occasions to bless His name for His preventing goodness when we are in the midst of evil.

Fourth, Christ protects us in His ways and does not allow us to relapse from Him into a state of sin and bondage to Satan. Indeed, Satan is restless in his endeavors to reduce us again to his obedience. He never stops tempting and soliciting us. But Christ keeps His own (John 17:12). We are "kept by the power of God through faith unto salvation" (1 Peter 1:5). We are "preserved in Jesus Christ" (Jude 1).

Fifth, Christ rewards our obedience and encourages our sincere service. Though all we do for Christ is duty, He has united our comfort with our duty. We are engaged to take the following encouragement with us to every duty: He whom we seek "is a rewarder of them that diligently seek him" (Heb. 11:6).

Sixth, Christ pacifies all inward troubles and commands peace when our souls are tumultuous. This peace rules in our hearts (Col. 3:15). When tumultuous affections are in a hurry, when anger, hatred, and revenge begin to rise in the soul, this peace hushes and stills all. He who says to the raging sea, "Be still," can calm the disquieted spirit.

These are Christ's kingly acts. And He puts them forth upon the souls of His people. (1) He does so *powerfully*. Whether He restrains from sin or impels to duty, He does it with determining efficacy (1 Cor. 4:20). (2) He does so *sweetly*. He does not rule by compulsion. His law is a law of love, written upon our hearts. "A bruised reed shall he not break, and the smoking flax shall he not quench" (Isa. 42:3). He rules children, not slaves, and so His kingly power is mixed with fatherly love. (3) He does so *suitably*. He rules us according to our natures in a rational way (Hos. 11:4), meaning He convinces our reason.

The Privilege of Christ's Rule

We will now open the privileges pertaining to all the subjects of this spiritual kingdom. First, we are fully and certainly set free from the curse of the law. "If the Son therefore shall make you free, ye shall be free indeed" (John 8:36). We are not free from the law as a rule of life, but free from its rigorous demands and terrible curses. To hear our liberty proclaimed from this bondage is indeed a joyful sound—the most blessed voice that our ears have ever heard (Gal. 5:18).

Second, we are free from the dominion of sin (Rom. 6:14). When Christ takes the throne, sin abandons it. It is true that the being of sin is still there and that its defiling and troubling power still remains, but its dominion is abolished.

Third, we are protected in all the troubles and dangers to which our souls and bodies are exposed. "Those that thou gavest me I have kept, and none of them is lost" (John 17:12).

Fourth, we have a king who meekly and tenderly bears our burdens and infirmities (Matt. 11:29; 21:5). He has compassion upon the ignorant and those who are out of the way.

Fifth, we enjoy sweet peace and tranquility of soul (Rom. 14:17). I do not say that we have actual peace at all times, but that we have the root and cause of peace. We have that which is convertible into peace at any time.

Sixth, we possess everlasting salvation. The kingdom of grace raises children for the kingdom of glory. The difference between the two is only gradual, and therefore both bear the name of the kingdom of heaven. The King is the same, and the subjects are the same. The subjects of this kingdom are shortly to be translated to that kingdom.

Application

Lesson 1

It is a great sin and misery to continue in bondage to sin and Satan and refuse Christ's government. Satan writes his laws in the blood of his subjects, grinds them with cruel oppression, wears them out with bondage to various lusts, and rewards their service with everlasting misery. And yet few people are weary of it and willing to come over to Christ. When will sinners be weary of their bondage and long for deliverance? If any poor soul reads these lines, let him know that Christ will not reject him (John 6:37). Come, poor sinner, come! Christ is a merciful king, and He has never rejected a poor, penitent sinner who submits to His mercy.

Lesson 2

It concerns us to know whose government we are under, and who is king over our souls—whether Christ or Satan is on the throne. To help us in this great work, we must make use of the following questions. First, do we obey Christ? We are the subject and servant of whomever we obey (Rom. 6:16). It is a mockery to give Christ the empty titles of *Lord* and *King* while we give our real service to sin and Satan. "Ye are my friends, if ye do whatsoever I command you" (John 15:14). Our obedience must be sincere and universal. This will evidence our sincere subjection to Christ (Rom. 12:2).

Second, do we have the power of godliness or a mere form of it? Many people trifle in religion, but they do not concern themselves with the power of religion and the life of godliness, which promote holiness and consist in communion with God in duties and ordinances. But surely "the kingdom of God is not in word, but in power" (1 Cor. 4:20).

Third, do we have the special saving knowledge of Christ? All His subjects are translated out of the kingdom of darkness (Col. 1:13). The devil is called the ruler of the darkness of this world. His subjects are all blind, else he could never rule them. But as soon as their eyes are opened, they run out of his kingdom, and there is no retaining them in subjection to him any longer. Have we been brought out of darkness into this marvelous light? Do we see our condition—how sad, miserable, and wretched it is by nature? Do we see our remedy, as it lies only in Christ and His precious blood? Do we see the true way of obtaining interest in that blood by faith? Does this knowledge turn into practice, causing us to repent of our sins, thirst after Christ's righteousness, and strive for a heart to believe and close with Christ?

Fourth, do we delight to associate with Christ's subjects? Who are our chosen companions? What business do the subjects of Christ have among the slaves of Satan? I know the subjects of both kingdoms are here mingled, and we cannot avoid the company of sinners except we go out of the world, but our delights ought to be in the saints.

Fifth, do we live a holy and righteous life? If not, we may claim interest in Christ as our king, but He will never acknowledge our claim. "The sceptre of thy kingdom is a right sceptre" (Ps. 45:6).

Lesson 3
We should walk as subjects of the King. The examples of kings are very influential upon their subjects. Our King has commanded us not only to take His yoke upon us but to learn of Him (Matt. 11:29). We are to walk as He walked (1 John

2:6). Our King is meek and patient (Isa. 53:7), humble and lowly (Matt. 21:5). Our King denied His outward comforts, ease, honor, and life to serve His Father's design and accomplish our salvation (Phil. 2:1–8). Our king was laborious and diligent in fulfilling His work (John 9:4). We must imitate our King, follow the pattern of our King. This will give us comfort now and boldness in the day of judgment (1 John 4:17).

17

The King's Providential Reign

And hath put all things under his feet, and gave him to be the head over all things to the church.
—EPHESIANS 1:22

In the preceding verses, the apostle Paul adores God's grace in bringing the Ephesians to believe in Christ. This effect of the power that raised their hearts to believe in Christ is here compared with that other glorious effect of it—Christ's resurrection. God's power raised Christ from a low estate, even from the dead, to a very high and glorious state—to be the head of the world and the church. He is the head of the world by way of dominion and the head of the church by way of union and special influence, ruling the world for the good of His people. "[He] gave him to be the head over all things to the church." It is important to notice four things in this verse.

First, the *nature* of this authority: "[He] hath put all things under his feet." This implies absolute dominion, which the Father has delegated to Christ. In addition to the essential power and dominion that is common to every person in the Godhead (Ps. 22:28), there is a mediatory authority that is proper to Christ. He received it as the reward of His suffering (Phil. 2:8–9).

Second, the *subject* of this authority: "Christ." He is the only recipient of all power and authority. The authority of the creature (political and ecclesiastical) is but derivative and ministerial. Christ is the only Lord—the fountain of all power (Jude 4).

Third, the object of this authority: "over all things." This is the whole creation. Christ rules from sea to sea. "Thou hast given him power over all flesh" (John 17:2)—all creatures (rational and irrational, animate and inanimate). All angels, devils, humans, winds, and seas obey Him.

Fourth, the *end* of this authority: "to be head over all things to the church." Christ governs the universe for the church's comfort, advantage, and salvation. God the Father has put all things into Christ's hand, to order and dispose all things as He pleases. As He purchased the persons of some, so He purchased the services of all. They now serve the end for which they were designed. Christ orders all of them in a blessed subordination to His purposes.

Doctrine: Christ orders and determines all the affairs of the kingdom of providence for the special advantage and everlasting good of His redeemed people.

"As thou hast given him power over all flesh, that he should give eternal life to as many as thou hast given him" (John 17:2). Hence it comes to pass that "all things work together for good to them that love God, to them who are the called according to his purpose" (Rom. 8:28). Christ's providential influence upon all the world's affairs is clearly evident from Scripture. My business is to show how He administers His kingdom.

The Means of Christ's Rule
Christ rules and orders the kingdom of providence by supporting, permitting, restraining, limiting, protecting, punishing, and rewarding those over whom He reigns. First, Christ supports the world, and all creatures in it, by His power (Col. 1:17). It is a considerable part of Christ's glory to have a whole world of creatures owing their creation and preservation to Him.

Second, Christ permits the worst of creatures in His dominion to exist and act as they do (Job 12:16). Even those who fight against Christ and His people receive power and permission from Him. He permits no more than He will overrule to His praise; therefore, His permission of evil is holy and just. Christ's working is not confounded with the creatures' working. His holiness has no fellowship with their iniquities, nor are their transgressions excused by His permission of them (Deut. 32:4–5). This holy permission is but the withholding of those restraints from their lusts and the denying of those common assistances that He is in no way bound to give them (Acts 14:16). If He were to permit sinful creatures to act out all the wickedness that is in their hearts, there would be neither peace nor order in the world.

Third, Christ restrains creatures from the commission of those things to which their hearts are inclined (Ps. 76:10). He lets forth as much evil as serves His holy ends. This is one of the glorious mysteries of providence, which amazes the serious and considerate soul—to see a creature determined to do mischief, with power to do it and with opportunity to do it, yet strangely hindered. See Laban (Gen. 31:24) and Sennacherib (2 Kings 19:7–8).

Fourth, Christ limits the creatures in their actions, assigning them boundaries that they cannot pass (Rev. 2:10).

Fifth, Christ protects His people in a world of enemies and dangers. They are "preserved in Jesus Christ" (Jude 1) as Noah and his family were preserved in the ark.

Sixth, Christ punishes evil doers, and repays them for their evil. Pharaoh, Sennacherib, and many more are the lasting monuments of Christ's righteous retribution. Christ rules with a rod of iron in the midst of His enemies (Ps. 110:2).

Seventh, Christ rewards the services done to Him and His people. He often repays those who serve Him out of His treasure of providence.

The Manner of Christ's Rule

There is not a creature in heaven, earth, or hell that Christ cannot use to serve His ends and promote His designs. Whatever the instrument, His manner of working remains the same. First, it is *holy*. Though He permits, limits, orders, and overrules unholy people and actions, He still works in purity and holiness. "The LORD is righteous in all his ways, and holy in all his works" (Ps. 145:17). It is easier to separate light from a sunbeam than holiness from God's works.

Second, it is *wise*. The rings are "full of eyes" (Ezek. 1:18). They are not moved by a blind impetus, but by deep counsel. The wisdom of providence manifests itself principally in the choice of such states for God's people as will most effectually promote their eternal happiness. This goes well beyond our comprehension. Providence looks beyond us. It eyes the end and suits all things to it, not to our fond desires.

Third, it is *supreme*. "Whatsoever the LORD pleased, that did he in heaven, and in earth, in the seas, and all deep places" (Ps. 135:6). He is "KING OF KINGS, AND LORD OF LORDS" (Rev. 19:16). The greatest monarchs on earth are but as little bits of clay (Prov. 8:15–16).

Fourth, it is *profound*. The judgments of Christ are "a great deep" (Ps. 36:6). There are hard texts in the works as well as in the words of Christ. The wisest minds have been at a loss in interpreting providence (Jer. 12:1–2).

Fifth, it is *irresistible*. All providences are the accomplishment of God's immutable decrees (Eph. 1:11). When the Jews put Christ to death, they did what God's "hand and…counsel determined before to be done" (Acts 4:28). No one can oppose or resist providence (Isa. 43:13).

Sixth, it is *harmonious*. There are secret chains and invisible connections between the works of Christ. We do not know how to reconcile His promises and providences, but certainly they all work together (Rom. 8:28). He does not undo or destroy one providence with another. As all seasons of the year, the nipping frosts of winter as well as the halcyon days of summer, contribute to the harvest, so it is in providence.

Seventh, it is *good*. Christ's providential kingdom is subordinate to His spiritual kingdom. "[He] is the Saviour of all men, specially of those that believe" (1 Tim. 4:10). They alone have the blessing of providence. Christ so orders all things that they serve for the eternal good of His people.

Application

Lesson 1

We are indebted to Christ for our lives, comforts, liberties, and all that we enjoy in this world. Christ governs everything for us. He is in heaven, out of sight, but He sees us and takes care of all our concerns. "In all thy ways acknowledge him" (Prov. 3:6). He sees when we are in danger by temptation and orders a protecting providence to hinder it. He sees when we are grieved and orders a reviving providence to refresh us. He sees when corruptions prevail and orders a humbling providence to cleanse us. Whatever mercies we have received all along the way are the orderings of Christ for us.

Lesson 2

We can leave our particular concerns in Christ's hands and know that the infinite love and wisdom, which rule the world, manage everything that relates to us. Our lives are in good hands, and infinitely better than if they were in our own. It is none of our business to steer the course of providence, but to submit quietly to Him who does. There is an itch in us to dispute with God (Jer. 12:1–2). We tend to complain of providence, as if it did not concern God's glory and our good. We also tend to distrust providence, as if it could never accomplish what we claim to expect and believe. There are but few Abrahams among us, who "against hope believed in hope… giving glory to God" (Rom. 4:18, 20). It is too common for us to fret and repine at providence, when our wills or lusts are crossed by it. These things ought not to be so. We need to confess our folly and ignorance (Ps. 73:22). And we need to consider the design of providence, which is to bring about

God's gracious purposes for us. This would quickly shape our hearts into a better and quieter frame.

Lesson 3

We do not need to stand in fear of creatures. Christ, our head and husband, is the Lord of all the hosts of heaven and earth. No creature can move its hand or tongue without His permission. Their power is given to them from above (John 19:11–12). The serious consideration of this truth will make the feeblest soul to cease trembling. He has given us abundant security in His promises: "All things work together for good to them that love God" (Rom. 8:28). Our relation to the King should be sufficient security, for He is the universal, supreme, absolute, meek, merciful, victorious, and immortal king. He sits in glory at the Father's right hand. His enemies are a footstool for Him. His love for His people is unspeakably tender and fervent. He who touches them "toucheth the apple of his eye" (Zech. 2:8). It is unimaginable that Christ will sit still while His enemies seek to thrust out His eyes. He loves us too well to sign any order to our prejudice, and without His order nothing can touch us.

Lesson 4

We can entrust all our affairs to Christ. This is the way to ensure their success and prosperity. If everything depends upon His pleasure, then it is wise to take Him along with us to every action and business. Time spent in prayer, when we seek His presence and ask His permission, is not lost time. We may take it for a clear truth: that which is not prefaced with prayer will be followed with trouble.

Lesson 5

We should look to Christ in all the events of providence. His hand is in everything that befalls us, whether it is evil or good (Ps. 111:2). In all the evil that befalls us, in trouble and affliction, we must look to Christ and set our hearts to study these four things. (1) Christ's *dominion*. He creates and forms trouble and affliction. They do not rise out of the dust, nor do they befall us casually, but He raises them up and gives them their commission (Jer. 18:11). He elects the instrument of our trouble; He makes the rod as afflictive as He pleases; He orders the continuance and end of our troubles. (2) Christ's *wisdom*. It is evident in how He chooses the trouble that is most apt to work upon us, purging out the corruption that dominates us. (3) Christ's *compassion*. There is mercy in His support under affliction and in His deliverance out of affliction. (4) Christ's *love*. If He did not love us, He would not sanctify a rod to humble us; rather, He would leave us alone to perish in our sin (Rev. 3:19). This is the design of His love: to recover us to our God and prevent our ruin.

In all the good that befalls us, we must look to Christ and consider the loveliness of the mercies we enjoy. (1) Their *suitableness*. Christ orders all things conveniently for us. If we had more of the world, it would be like a large sail to a little boat, which would quickly pull us under water. We have what is most suitable to our condition. (2) Their *reasonableness*. They are timed to an hour. Providence brings forth all its fruits in due season. (3) Their *nature*. We have a double sweetness in our enjoyments—one is natural (from the matter of it) and one is spiritual (from the end for which it comes). (4) Their *order*. One mercy is strangely linked to another, and each is a door to let in many. Sometimes one mercy is but an introduction to a thousand. (5) Their *constancy*. "They are new every morning" (Lam. 3:23). If there were a suspension of Christ's care for only one hour, it would be our ruin. Thousands of evils stand around us, watching to see if Christ will remove His eye from us, so that they can rush in and devour us.

Could we thus study Christ's providence in all the good and evil that befalls us in the world, then we would be content in every condition (Phil. 4:11), we would be furthered in our way by all that happens, and we would answer all Christ's ends in every state into which He brings us. We should do this, and say, "Thanks be to God for Jesus Christ!"

Conclusion

Reader, in a little while, you will come to the last day of your life. Do you have an interest in this blessed Redeemer? There is no sadder sight than a poor Christless sinner shivering upon the brink of eternity. "Lord, what will become of me?" That this may not be your case, reflect upon what you have read in these sermons. Judge yourself in the light of them. Obey the calls of the Holy Spirit in them. Let not your slight and formal spirit float upon the surface of these truths, like a feather upon the water. Get them deeply fixed upon your soul by the Spirit of the Lord, turning them into life and power within you, so animating the whole course of your life that it may proclaim that you are one who esteems everything as dross that you may win Christ.

11/3/22